Healthy Eating
for Your Heart

Paul Gayler   Jacqui Lynas B.Sc. R.D.

Healthy Eating for Your Heart

photography by Peter Cassidy

BARNES
&NOBLE
BOOKS
NEW YORK

Breakfasts and
Brunches 41

Soups and Salads 53

Light Meals and
Appetizers 71

Main Courses 89

Desserts 141

This edition published by Barnes & Noble Inc., by arrangement with Kyle Cathie Ltd

2004 Barnes & Noble Books

M 10 9 8 7 6 5 4 3 2 1

ISBN 0-7607-5340-7

First published in Great Britain in 2003 by Kyle Cathie Ltd

Paul Gayler and Jacqui Lynas are hereby identified as the authors of this work in accordance with Section 77 of the Copyright, Designs, and Patents Act 1988.

Text © 2003 Paul Gayler and Jacqui Lynas
Photography © 2003 Peter Cassidy
Book design © 2003 Kyle Cathie Limited

Senior Editor: Muna Reyal
Designer: Carl Hodson
Photographer: Peter Cassidy
Home economist: Linda Tubby
Styling: Penny Markham
Copy editor: Anne Newman
Recipe analysis: Dr. Wendy Doyle
Production: Sha Huxtable

A Cataloguing In Publication record for this title is available from the British Library.

Color reproduction by Sang Choy
Printed and bound in Singapore by Star Standard

Important note

The information and advice contained in this book are intended as a general guide to healthy eating and are not specific to individuals or their particular circumstances. This book is not intended to replace treatment by a qualified doctor or medical professional. Neither the authors nor the publishers can be held responsible for claims arising from the inappropriate use of any dietary regime. Do not attempt self-diagnosis or self-treatment for serious or long-term conditions without consulting a medical professional or qualified doctor.

'To Anita and family'
Home is where the heart is. P.G.

To my husband, Dr. Jonathan Morrell, for his love, encouragement, and help, and my dear children Lottie, Sam, and Tom, for their continuing patience – with much love and thanks. J.L.

Books that are written with you, the cook, in mind, are a joy to read and use – here is one such publication that fits that bill perfectly. At the same time, it helps to address the concerns that we should all have about eating with health in mind.

H·E·A·R·T UK is a registered UK charity that works to raise awareness of heart disease, while promoting the importance of a healthy lifestyle. Much of our time as a charity is spent being concerned about those who need to eat healthily – it is to those people, many of them with inherited high cholesterol, that we suggest eating healthily as their "first change for the better."

105 million Americans have a total cholesterol of 200mg/dL or higher, a level at which cardiovascular risk begins to rise. Many of these people have familial hypercholesterolaemia (FH), the inherited condition characterized by high cholesterol levels, and they have to be particularly careful about what they eat. For most, drug therapy will be part of their daily lives, but the help, advice, and counseling of charities like H·E·A·R·T UK can show them that dull and boring food need not be on their menus.

Millions of others do not have FH, but have an inherited predisposition to high cholesterol. So it is equally important that we all benefit from a change for the better; and what better way than diving into these pages and reinventing the best of food for your table, your family, and their better heart health?

Much of what you, the cook and reader, can do about helping to reduce the risk of heart disease in your family is described here between the covers of this book – without compromising the looks and taste of your food. Here particularly, the result is at the opposite end of the spectrum: variety, spice, and excitement are included in all the ingredients and thus, the repast!

Pleasurable page upon pleasurable page – and the recipes on each leaf turned are utterly good for you! Enjoy yourselves and enjoy your food!

If you would like to know more about the work of H·E·A·R·T UK, please contact the charity by mail (7 North Road, Maidenhead, Berkshire SL6 1PE, England), telephone (011 44 (0)1628 628 638), e-mail (ask@heartuk.org.uk), or visit our website (www.heartuk.org.uk).

Introduction

Cardiovascular disease (CVD) is the number one killer in the world, with twelve million deaths each year, a figure that is increasing annually. CVD is a collective term which includes not only coronary heart disease (CHD), but also stroke, and all other diseases of the heart and circulation. In the US, CVD claims more lives each year than the next five leading causes of death, which are cancer, chronic lower respiratory diseases, accidents, diabetes mellitus, and influenza and pneumonia. Nearly 2,600 Americans die from CVD each day – an average of one every 33 seconds. A common myth about CVD is that it mostly affects men, but in fact it claims the lives of more than half a million women every year – about one a minute. It is not a disease that affects just older people either, since CVD ranks as the second most common cause of death, behind accidents, in children under 15.

Long-term effects

These alarming statistics are only part of the story, since heart disease is also a major cause of ill health which can be debilitating, significantly affecting a sufferer's quality of life. In the US, approximately seven million people suffer from angina, five million from heart failure, and there are around eight million heart attacks per year, about half of which are fatal. Even for those lucky enough to survive a heart attack, life is never quite the same again.

Heart disease has developed into a common lethal epidemic and we are all likely to know someone – a member of the family, a friend, or colleague – who has been touched by this disease. The tragedy is further compounded when heart disease and heart attacks are premature, cheating the victim of either a healthy quality of life or their natural life expectancy.

Changing your life

On a brighter note, the good news is that heart disease is potentially avoidable and preventable. Most of the risk factors for heart disease can be reduced by following a healthy lifestyle. In essence, this means not smoking, doing plenty of physical activity, maintaining a sensible weight, and choosing a healthy diet. Even if you already have heart disease, it is never too late to change your ways, and the onset of symptoms is a particularly good time for you to reassess your lifestyle.

Heart food

A healthy diet can have a positive influence on the majority of risk factors for heart disease, which include high cholesterol levels, high blood pressure, being overweight, and having diabetes. It is estimated that up to 30 percent of deaths from heart disease are due to unhealthy diet. Using sound scientific research as well as consensus opinion, nutritional experts have identified several inter-related, multi-faceted strategies for eating for a healthy heart. Latest advice highlights the overall benefits of a varied diet which, while low in fat, has the right balance of different fats, includes an abundance of plant foods, and is low in salt. However, the effects of diet are very complex and although there have been some remarkable discoveries in recent years, there is still much to explore.

The emerging picture is that in order to protect against heart disease, we should adopt a dietary pattern similar to that traditionally eaten in Mediterranean and Asian countries. The key to good heart protection is to eat fresh foods: plenty of fruit, vegetables and salads, fish, whole grains, beans, nuts and seeds, together with moderate amounts of lean meat and low-fat dairy foods. These dietary recommendations are in line with others which help people to enjoy healthy eating for the prevention of cancer, diabetes, and obesity.

About Heart Disease

Heart disease or, more specifically, coronary heart disease is caused by a hardening or narrowing of the arteries which surround the heart. These blood vessels supply fuel and oxygen to the heart muscle, allowing it to pump blood to all the organs in the body. Aging, poor diet, and an unhealthy lifestyle cause fatty, cholesterol-laden deposits to form in the smooth artery linings, a process which can even begin in childhood.

Angina

Angina is often the first sign of heart disease, signaled by pain across the chest but sometimes in the shoulders, arms, throat, or jaw. The narrowed coronary arteries reduce the rate at which blood can be delivered to the beating heart muscle. The pain is usually a heavy or tight one, generally lasting for under ten minutes. Angina commonly occurs with strenuous activity, as this makes the heart beat faster and increases its need for energy and oxygen. The discomfort of angina occurs more readily in cold, windy weather, after eating a large meal, or with excitement or stress. Rest, relaxation, and, for some, using angina medication usually bring relief in a few minutes. The situation becomes more serious when angina occurs at rest or with minimal activity, or comes on with increasing frequency or severity.

Heart attack

A heart attack occurs suddenly when a blood clot forms in a narrowed coronary artery, completely blocking blood flow, and thereby causing an area of the heart muscle to die. Commonly, the pain is severe and crushing, lasting for longer than fifteen minutes, and not relieved by rest. The outcome depends on the site and size of the artery involved, and the affected area of the heart muscle. When only a small area is involved, there is a good chance of a full recovery. However, if larger areas are involved, the heart attack may prove fatal, or result in an incomplete recovery since the heart muscle loses some of its power and strength. Sometimes the heart will stop altogether, or abnormal heart-beat rhythms (arrhythmias) take over, and both of these scenarios can cause sudden death.

Stroke

Most incidences of stroke occur in a similar way to heart attacks, but the arteries concerned are those that supply the brain. Stroke occurs when part of the brain has been deprived of blood flow, usually because of a sudden blockage in the artery caused by a blood clot. "Mini-strokes" can occur when the brain is briefly deprived of its blood supply but manages to recover within minutes. People who have had heart attacks are at increased risk of stroke, and vice versa.

Classic Risk Factors for Coronary Heart Disease

Some you cannot change:
- Age – the older you are, the greater the risk
- Male sex – women are at lower risk before the menopause
- Family history – especially heart disease in a close relative under 55 years old

Some that can be reduced, controlled, or eliminated:
- High blood cholesterol
- High blood pressure
- Diabetes
- Being overweight
- Smoking
- Lack of physical activity

Reducing Risks

Cholesterol

This is a soft white waxy substance that is essential to health since it is a building block for all cell membranes, bile salts, vitamin D, and various hormones. Cholesterol is only a problem if you have too much of it since this can increase your risk of heart disease. Cholesterol comes from two sources. The majority is made in the body, mostly in the liver from saturated fat, but it is also found in foods that are obtained from animals, such as fatty meats, poultry, fish, seafood, eggs, and dairy products.

A 10 percent decrease in total cholesterol levels may result in an estimated 30 percent reduction in the incidence of CHD. The American Heart Association's Nutrition Committee strongly advises that healthy Americans over the age of two limit their intake of saturated fat to 7–10 percent of total Calories.

"Good" and "bad" cholesterol

Cholesterol is transported in the bloodstream in tiny "carriers" called lipoproteins. The types of carrier are classified by their density, the two most important carriers being low-density lipoprotein (LDL) and high-density lipoprotein (HDL). Most of the blood cholesterol is carried from the liver to the body's tissues in low-density lipoproteins and is therefore called low-density lipoprotein cholesterol or LDL cholesterol. A high level of this increases your risk of heart disease. This is because, in modified forms, it can slowly build up in the walls of coronary arteries, forming "atherosclerotic plaques," the fatty deposits that narrow the arteries and ultimately cause angina and heart attacks. To simplify matters, LDL cholesterol is often called "bad" cholesterol, and the lower it is, the better.

Conversely, cholesterol carried in high-density lipoproteins is called HDL cholesterol. HDL cholesterol is thought of as "good" cholesterol, since high levels reduce the risk of heart disease, and low levels increase the risk of heart disease. HDL cholesterol seems to act as a "biological vacuum cleaner," removing cholesterol from the body cells, including artery walls, and returning it to the liver for excretion. The higher your HDL cholesterol, the lower will be your risk of heart disease.

Triglycerides

Triglycerides are the most common form of fat, both in the diet and in the human body, and are often stored subcutaneously just where we don't want them! Most of the triglycerides, a different kind of fat from cholesterol, are carried in very low density lipoprotein (VLDL). These particles also contain small amounts of cholesterol which can be deposited in the wall of the artery, increasing the risk of heart disease. Very high levels of triglycerides can cause pancreatitis. High blood triglyceride levels are often seen in people who are overweight, have type 2 diabetes, or drink too much alcohol. Research has shown that even if your cholesterol level is normal, if you have a high level of triglycerides and a low level of HDL cholesterol, you may still be at increased risk of heart disease. Keeping fit, slim, and enjoying a healthy diet which includes oily fish or fish oil, keeps triglyceride levels under control.

What are lipids?

Lipids are the collective name for fatty substances in the blood. If you want to know your levels, you will need to have a blood test. A fasting blood test (where you fast for 12–16 hours, drinking only water) will tell you the level of both LDL and HDL cholesterol, as well as your level of triglycerides. A random, non-fasting test measures just the total and HDL cholesterol.

What is a good lipid pattern?

The average cholesterol level of most people in the westernized world is 5.9 mmol/L (225mg/dL), yet in areas of rural China, the average cholesterol level is 3.0mmol/L (115mg/dL) and the rate of heart disease in those places is very low.

Reasonable targets to aim for are:
- Total cholesterol level below 5.0mmol/L (195mg/dL)
- LDL cholesterol level below 3.0mmol/L (115mg/dL)
- HDL cholesterol above 0.9mmol/L (35mg/dL)
- Triglyceride level below 1.5mmol/L (57mg/dL)

It is likely that the lower the cholesterol level, the better. If you can keep your cholesterol level below 5mmol/L (195mg/dL) for two years, there is a good chance that any atheroma, which has already been deposited, might regress or stabilize.

If you already have heart disease or are at high risk of developing it, your doctor may have prescribed medication to modify your lipid levels. The benefits of these drugs are significant, and their effect is enhanced by a healthy diet.

High blood pressure

Everybody has – and needs – blood pressure. A certain amount of blood pressure is vital to keep blood flowing through the arteries, delivering energy and oxygen to all parts of the body. Blood pressure is only harmful if it becomes too high, usually as a result of the arteries losing their elasticity. As the heart beats, blood is pumped into the arteries and a pressure is created, which causes blood to circulate through the body. When your blood pressure is measured, two numbers are recorded, for example 120/60 mmHg (millimetres of mercury). The top number (systolic pressure) measures the pressure in your arteries when the heart beats. The bottom number (diastolic pressure) measures the pressure while your heart rests between beats.

There is much discussion about what constitutes "normal" blood pressure, but the table below shows the most recent recommendations (high normal is the highest "normal" value before it becomes abnormal).

Your blood pressure can change from minute to minute because of changes in posture, exercise, or when sleeping, and therefore several readings should be taken over a period of time, before a decision is made about blood pressure.

Normal blood pressure should be less than 140/90 mmHg. If you have heart disease, it should be less than 140/85 mmHg, and even lower if you have diabetes or kidney disease because of the higher risk of heart disease associated with these conditions.

If your blood pressure constantly measures above 140/90 mmHg, you have high blood pressure or hypertension. This adds to the workload of your heart and arteries. The heart must therefore work harder than normal and this may cause it to enlarge. As you grow older, your arteries will harden and become less elastic, and high blood pressure speeds up this process. High blood pressure can be controlled by a combination of healthy eating, physical activity, and medication. A cardio-protective dietary pattern, avoiding salt, reducing alcohol, and keeping slim have all been shown to reduce blood pressure.

Diabetes

Diabetes is on the increase worldwide, currently affecting 2.1 percent of the world's population (or 124 million people). It is estimated that for every person who has been diagnosed, there is another walking around undiagnosed and therefore untreated. Diabetes type 1 develops when the body produces little or no insulin, and is treated by insulin injections and a healthy balanced diet. Type 2 is the most common type of diabetes and develops when the body can still make its own insulin, but not enough for its needs, or when the insulin that the body does make is not used properly. It is treated by a healthy diet or a healthy diet and tablets. Type 2 is linked to obesity, especially when there is excess weight around the stomach; as obesity increases worldwide, so does the time bomb of type 2 diabetes. Alarmingly, the fuse has been lit even in the younger generation

Blood pressure recommendations

	SYSTOLIC BLOOD PRESSURE mmHG	DIASTOLIC BLOOD PRESSURE mmHG
Optimal	Less than 120	Less than 80
Normal	Less than 130	Less than 85
High normal	130–139	85–89

who are developing type 2 diabetes in their teens because they are overweight, as a result of a poor diet and also a lack of physical activity.

Heart disease is the leading cause of death for people with diabetes and accounts for 50 percent of all deaths. Reducing risk factors is particularly important for people with diabetes.

Maintaining a good weight

Obesity rates have almost tripled in the past 20 years, and if current trends continue, at least one in four adults will be obese by 2010. Obesity is related to other risk factors for heart disease – higher blood pressure, higher blood cholesterol levels, and increased risk of type 2 diabetes. The good news is that even modest weight loss (five-to-ten percent of initial weight) is linked to significant health benefits.

Are you apple- or pear-shaped?

It is not just being overweight that is the problem, but where the weight is deposited. There is an association between body shape and heart disease, such that people who are "pear-shaped", with fat deposited over their hips and thighs, seem to be at much lower risk than those who are "apple-shaped," with fat carried around the front, like a "pot" or "beer" belly. Fat cells deposited over the abdomen make the body more insulin resistant, resulting in a classic clustering of risk factors, called the insulin- resistance syndrome. More

Waist measurements

	AIM FOR:	AT INCREASED RISK – YOUR HEALTH COULD SUFFER. DON'T PUT ON MORE WEIGHT.	AT SUBSTANTIAL RISK – YOUR HEALTH IS AT RISK. SEEK ADVICE ON LOSING WEIGHT.
Women	Less than 31½"	More than 31½"	More than 34½"
Men	Less than 37"	More than 37"	More than 40"

insulin is produced, which increases the tendency to diabetes, increases blood pressure, cholesterol, and triglycerides, lowers HDL cholesterol, and increases the tendency for the blood to form clots. Health professionals are increasingly using waist measurement rather than weight to identify people at risk of heart disease. Check your own shape by measuring your waist with a tape measure (midway between the lowest ribs and hip-bone).

Smoking

Smoking is a major cause of heart disease. People who smoke cigarettes have twice the risk of developing coronary heart disease as those who do not. For those under 50 years, the risk is 10 times greater than for non-smokers of the same age. The good news is that stopping smoking carries an almost immediate benefit, and the risks of smoking reduce progressively after stopping. If you smoke, you should get help to quit! Even passive smoking increases the risk of heart disease significantly. Smoking also increases the risk of cancer and lung disease.

Lack of physical activity

Many people do not engage in any physical activity during a typical week. Physical inactivity roughly doubles the risk of heart disease and is a major risk factor for stroke. Accumulating evidence suggests that regular activity such as brisk walking, cycling, dancing, or gardening are useful for the prevention and treatment of heart disease, stroke, diabetes, obesity, and osteoporosis. Recent research also suggests that even everyday movement results in other benefits including cushioning the effects of stress, alleviating and preventing depression, reducing levels of anxiety, and improving self-esteem. It is recommended that you should walk, cycle, or swim for 30 minutes on at least five days of the week, and if you don't have 30 minutes to spare, try to do 15 minutes twice or 10 minutes three times a day. Such activities should leave you feeling warm and slightly out of breath.

Take it slowly at first; there is no need to exhaust yourself. Walking is a great exercise to start with as it provides all the exercise your heart needs, and you can build it up gradually, increasing the distance and pace little by little.

The Cardioprotective Diet

In the 1960s, epidemiologist Dr. Ancel Keys, and his colleagues, examined the relationship between diet and heart disease rates in seven countries and found that people who lived along the Mediterranean Sea suffered only a tiny fraction of the heart attacks and coronary deaths experienced by Americans and people in Western industrialized countries. The dietary fat consumed by Mediterranean people was mostly of vegetable origin, in contrast to the diets rich in highly saturated animal fats from meat and dairy products consumed in other countries.

The population of Crete has the lowest rate of death from heart disease and the longest life expectancy of all the Mediterranean countries. A Cretan diet is rich in legumes, fruits, vegetables, olive oil, and red wine. The diet is also high in alpha-linolenic acid (see page 16) from wild plants, legumes, walnuts, figs, and snails, and much lower in linoleic acid (see page 16) than other Mediterranean diets. Interestingly, in terms of the essential fatty acid and antioxidant content (see page 22), the diet of Crete is similar to the Palaeolithic diet with which humans evolved over tens of thousands of years ago.

The term "Mediterranean diet" was coined in the cookbook *How to Eat Well*

What are the characteristics of a cardioprotective diet?

▸ Low in saturated fat

▸ High in monounsaturated fat (mainly olive oil)

▸ Balanced in omega-6 and omega-3 fatty acids

▸ Abundant in fruits and vegetables; rich in cardioprotective nutrients

▸ Based on a diet high in whole-grain cereals, vegetables, and legumes

▸ Includes moderate amounts of lean meat, fish, dairy foods, and eggs

and Stay Well, the Mediterranean Way written by Ancel and Margaret Keys in the late 1950s, promoting the delicious foods that happen to protect against heart disease and several common cancers.

The Mediterranean diet has now come to epitomize the cardioprotective diet. Other cultures have evolved diets of similar nutritional composition and they also have low rates of heart disease. The cuisines of many Asian countries provide such examples, and experts have coined the phrase the "Mediterrasian" diet.

Fats in the cardioprotective diet

Some fat is important in the diet since it is a provider of concentrated energy, an energy store, and necessary for thermal insulation. Fat is also a vehicle for the fat-soluble vitamins A, D, E, and K, and the "essential" fats, linoleic acid and alpha-linolenic acid, which cannot be made in the body. However, we eat too much fat, particularly saturated, which raises blood cholesterol and leads to heart disease. Recommended fat intakes are based on energy needs and physical activity levels. Present guidelines suggest that no more than 30 to 35 percent of daily energy intake should come from fat, and no more than 10 percent from saturated fat. The energy requirements for an average woman and man are 2,000 and 2,500 Calories per day, respectively (see table above).

In addition, some fats are more beneficial than others. There are three main types of fat in food – saturated, monounsaturated, and polyunsaturated. All fatty foods are made up from a mixture of the three, but are classified according to the type of fat present in the largest amount. Saturated fats are found mostly in animal products, and most are solid at room temperature; palm oil and coconut oil are non-animal and non-solid saturated fats. Monounsaturated fats are found in olive and rapeseed oils, and in spreads made from them. Polyunsaturated fats, often liquid at room temperature, are found in vegetable oils, such as sunflower, safflower, and in cereals, nuts, and seeds.

Saturated fat

Foods high in saturated fat are found mainly in meat and dairy produce, and are the major influence on the level of cholesterol in the blood. Cholesterol is made in the liver, and the amount produced is directly related to the amount of saturated fat in the diet. The more saturated fat we eat, the higher our blood cholesterol. On the other hand, foods which contain cholesterol have very little influence on blood cholesterol, even cholesterol-rich foods such as egg yolks, liver, sweetbreads, shrimp, and shellfish. This is because these foods contain relatively little saturated fat, not all of which is absorbed anyway. This means that the most important thing to look out for is the saturated fat content.

Trans fats are found in certain foods in small amounts, and behave much like saturated fats. They are found naturally in small amounts in meat and dairy products, but they are also formed when vegetable oils are hydrogenated to make solid fats for processed foods such as cakes, cookies, pastries, and fast foods.

Monounsaturated fat

When monounsaturated fat is used in place of saturated fat, blood cholesterol levels are lowered. Olive oil, a basic constituent of the Mediterranean diet, is rich in monounsaturates. It is preferable to all other oils since it is very low in omega-6 fatty acids, which give it a

Energy requirements

ENERGY INTAKE IN CALORIES	TOTAL FAT IN GRAMS	SATURATED FAT IN GRAMS
2,000	73	22
2,500	92	28

(Explanation of calculations: the percentage of energy derived from fat is 33 percent of 2,500, i.e., 825 Calories. There are 9 Calories in each gram of fat, so this equates to 825÷9 = 92g of fat).

	MAIN SOURCES	EFFECT ON RISK FACTORS
Saturated fats	Fatty meats and meat products, lard, drippings, suet; dairy products such as whole milk, cream, butter, and cheese. Coconut oil, palm kernel oil, and palm oil used in ready-made foods, cakes, cookies, etc.	Raise cholesterol
Trans fats	Found in small amounts in the fat of dairy products and some meats, but mainly in hydrogenated vegetable oils and in prepared foods such as cookies, etc.	Raise cholesterol

favorable ratio of omega-6 to omega-3 fatty acids (see below). In addition it is rich in antioxidants (see page 22) and contains a substance called squalene, which has anti-inflammatory properties, slows blood clot formation, and lowers cholesterol. Another good mono-unsaturated oil to use is rapeseed oil (canola), which is the oil used for most vegetable oils (always check the label).

Monounsaturated fatty acids are particularly beneficial since their chemical nature makes them resistant to oxidative changes. Olive oil has remarkable stability and can be stored for eighteen months and more. This resistance to the development of rancidity is combined with a marvelous variety of flavors and colors, allowing for a range of culinary applications with little or no processing. A simple traditional salad dressing can be created instantly by combining olive oil and fresh lemon juice, which creates a rich source of both

lipid-soluble and water-soluble vitamins. In salads or in cooking, olive oil is usually mixed with herbs and spices, which are also important elements of the cardio-protective diet. Herbs like oregano, rosemary, and thyme are rich sources of phenolic compounds with strong antioxidant activity. These herbs maintain the nutritional value of the food and enhance the shelf life of the product.

Polyunsaturated Fats – Omega-6 and Omega-3

There are two main families of polyunsaturated fatty acids: the omega-6 family, which are derived from the essential fatty acid linoleic acid, and the omega-3 family, derived from the essential fatty acid, alpha-linolenic acid. Omega-6 fatty acids are found mainly in seed oils and polyunsaturated spreads. Omega-3 fatty acids are in oily fish (marine sources) and in some seed oils and vegetables (plant sources).

Both omega-6 and omega-3 fatty acids reduce the risk of heart attacks but have different and important biological effects. Omega-6 fatty acids lower blood cholesterol levels while omega-3 fatty acids reduce the risk of blood clots and inflammation, and also prevent abnormal

	MAIN SOURCES	EFFECT ON RISK FACTORS
Monounsaturated fats	Olive oil, rapeseed oil (canola), peanut or groundnut oil, nuts and nut spreads, avocados	Lower cholesterol when used instead of saturated fat; good source of antioxidants

heart rhythms. Omega-3 fatty acids may also exert a beneficial effect on blood pressure and lower blood triglyceride levels. The balance between omega-6 and omega-3 fatty acids is crucial. The Western diet contains an abundance of omega-6 fats in vegetable oils and spreads, but not enough omega-3s, possibly because high amounts of omega-3 fatty acids are found in relatively few foods. Oily fish is the richest source of the long-chain omega-3 fatty acids – eicosapentanoic acid (EPA) and docosahexanoic acid (DHA).

Fish

One of the most extraordinary nutrition revelations in recent years has been the role of fish in preventing heart disease. Studies have shown that eating fish can avert potentially fatal disruption of heart rhythms, and reduce the thickness and stickiness of the blood, which in turn means less chance of a blood clot and the start of a heart attack. There is a lower incidence of heart attacks among people who eat fish regularly, such as the Japanese and Greenland Inuits, than among non-fish eaters. The British Food Standards Agency advises eating two servings of fish per week, one of which should be oil-rich (see table on page 18). It is recommended that people who have already suffered a heart attack eat two to three medium servings of oil-rich fish per week, or take a daily fish oil supplement of 1g EPA and DHA. For vegetarians, DHA produced by algae can be bought as a supplement.

	MAIN SOURCES	EFFECT ON RISK FACTORS
Polyunsaturated fatty acids		
Omega-6	Vegetable oils such as sunflower, safflower, soy, corn oil, and spreads	Lowers blood cholesterol
Omega-3	Oily fish, flaxseeds and oil (linseed), rapeseed (canola), soy oil, walnut oil and walnuts, green leafy vegetables	Reduces thrombosis, inflammation, and fatal arrhythmias. Reduces blood pressure and triglycerides

OIL-RICH FISH WHICH ARE HIGH IN OMEGA-3 FATTY ACIDS (EPA AND DHA)	
	OMEGA-3 (GRAMS PER AVERAGE PORTION)
Mackerel	4.5
Kippered herring	3.7
Fresh tuna	3.0
Trout	2.9
Kippered herring (canned)	2.7
Salmon	2.5
Herring (pickled)	2.2
Pilchards (canned in brine or tomato sauce)	1.8
Salmon (pink or red, canned)	1.4
Smoked salmon (lox)	1.3
Mackerel (canned in sauce or oil)	1.3
Sardines (canned)	1.2
Swordfish	1.1
Tuna (canned in oil)	0.7
Crab (canned in brine)	0.6
Cod	0.3
Tuna (canned in brine)	0.1

The amount of omega-3 in fish varies according to the seasons, and whether fish is wild or farmed.

Plant sources of omega-3

Alpha-linolenic acid, which is a plant source of omega-3 fatty acid, is found in some seed oils, for example, linseed, rapeseed, and soy, and in some nuts (particularly walnuts) and green leafy vegetables. The body can synthesize longer-chain EPA and DHA from alpha-linolenic acid but the conversion rate is slow. Therefore it is important to have both fish and plant sources of omega-3 fatty acids, to increase their intake, and to improve the balance between omega-3 and omega-6 fatty acids.

PLANT SOURCES OF OMEGA-3 FATTY ACIDS (ALPHA-LINOLENIC ACID)	
	OMEGA-3 (GRAMS PER AVERAGE PORTION)
Flaxseed and flaxseed oil (linseeds and linseed oil)	1.8
Walnuts	1.5
Walnut oil	1.3
Rapeseed oil (canola)	1.0
Soy oil	0.8
Vegetable oil, blended	0.7
Soy margarine	0.2
Spinach and leafy green veg	0.2
Vegetarian baked beans in tomato sauce	0.2
Peanuts	0.2
Corn oil	0.1
Olive oil	0.08
Bread rolls (white or wholewheat)	0.08
Almonds	0.04
Sweet potatoes	0.04
Green peppers	0.02

OTHER SOURCES OF OMEGA-3 FATTY ACIDS	
	OMEGA-3 (GRAMS PER AVERAGE PORTION)
Chicken, dark meat, roasted	0.33
Roast leg of lamb	0.24
Cheddar cheese	0.19
Whole milk	0.15
Chicken, light meat	0.13
Broiled bacon	0.12
Roast leg of pork	0.11
Roast beef	0.10
Boiled egg	0.06
Yogurt	0.01

Some chickens fed on a special diet produce eggs which contain 0.5g of omega-3 per egg. Meat and dairy products can contain a useful source of alpha-linolenic acid, especially if the animals are grass-fed.

Key action points

▶ The secret of low-fat cuisine is to replace most of the added fats and oils in your cooking with aromatic vegetables, herbs, and spices, which will provide fresher and more vibrant flavors. Try tomatoes, black olives, chiles, pepper, canned beans, eggplants, mushrooms, herbs and spices such as ginger, garlic, fresh cilantro, roasted cumin, seeds, vinegar, and citrus juices.

▶ Oils may be used in tiny amounts but every tablespoon contains 120 Calories, so cut down the amount you use as much as possible.

▶ The healthiest spread for bread is probably a drizzle of virgin olive oil.

▶ Butter contains too much saturated fat and there is a vast array of spreads and margarines to confuse you. Choose a spread with a low saturated fat content of under 15g of saturated fat per 100g.

▶ Avoid spreads with hydrogenated vegetable oils since these are as bad as saturated fats; spreads made from monounsaturated and polyunsaturated oils such as olive oil, sunflower, or soy oil are good choices.

▶ If you are trying to lose weight, choose a low-fat spread that contains 38g of total fat or less, per 100g.

▶ Spreads with added plant stanols and sterols (see page 26) are also effective in reducing blood cholesterol levels by about 10 percent.

Fruit and vegetables in the cardioprotective diet

The World Health Organization and other health bodies have recognized the importance of a diet containing fruit and vegetables. Epidemiological studies have repeatedly shown that populations whose diets include plenty of fruits and vegetables have lower rates of heart disease and cancer than those which don't. The World Health Organization recommendation is for at least five portions of fruit and vegetables a day where fresh, frozen, dried, and canned all count. On average, people in the US eat only 2.8 servings of fruit and vegetables per day, and 70 percent do not meet the recommended servings for fruit.

WHAT COUNTS AS A PORTION?	
Apple, orange, or banana	1 fruit
Very large fruit, e.g., melon, pineapple	1 large slice
Small fruit, e.g., plums, kiwis, satsumas	2 fruits
Raspberries, strawberries, grapes	1 cup
Fresh fruit salad, stewed or canned fruit	2–3 tablespoons
Dried fruit	½–1 tablespoon
Fruit juice	1 small glass
Vegetables, raw, cooked, frozen, or canned	2 tablespoons
Salad	1 dessert bowl

1 portion of fruit or vegetables is roughly the size of your clenched fist.

Although potatoes are a vegetable, they count as a starchy carbohydrate and not as a portion of fruit and vegetables.

ANTIOXIDANTS	GOOD SOURCES
Vitamin E	Nuts, wheat germ, vegetable oils (namely seed oils), margarine, eggs
Betacarotene	Highly colored fruits and vegetables such as carrots, broccoli, tomatoes, red peppers, and pumpkins
Lycopene (a carotenoid)	Tomatoes
Vitamin C	Citrus fruits and green leafy vegetables customarily eaten raw in Mediterranean countries, so avoiding loss of vitamin C through cooking

ANTIOXIDANT TRACE ELEMENTS	GOOD SOURCES
Selenium	Beans and lentils, Brazil nuts, oily fish, sesame seeds, soy, walnuts
Zinc	Almonds, berries, broccoli, hazelnuts, mangoes, pine nuts, pumpkin, sesame and sunflower seeds, soy and tofu, sweet potatoes, tomatoes, watercress

Antioxidants

Fruit and vegetables are rich in antioxidants, which work to maintain health and protect us from damage caused by free radicals, which can injure cells and tissues. The body produces free radicals in the normal course of energy production, but certain pollutants (chemicals, smoke, solar radiation) trigger the production of free radicals. LDL cholesterol is vulnerable to oxidation by free-radical attack and oxidized LDL cholesterol is much more toxic and likely to accumulate in the artery wall.

Antioxidants include vitamin E, vitamin C, betacarotene, selenium, and zinc. In addition, some non-nutrient substances have been shown to have strong antioxidant properties, and may play a protective role. These include polyphenols (found in wine, tea, and olive oil), organic sulphides (in garlic), and anthocyanins, responsible for the fabulous colors in fruits and vegetables.

Non-vitamin antioxidants

Trace elements and polyphenols are powerful antioxidants and are particularly abundant in the Mediterranean diet because of the high proportion of fruit and vegetables consumed.

Selenium is of particular interest, because it enters the food chain through plants at a rate dependent on selenium concentrations in the soil. For this reason, dietary selenium intake varies substantially across populations: the wheat grown in the US has a higher selenium content than that from Europe. It is important to seek out a range of good sources of selenium in the diet (see table on page 22). Three Brazil nuts a day would provide sufficient intake.

In the Mediterranean basin, as a result of the warm climate and the prolonged exposure of crops to sunlight radiation, some plant species such as olives, grapes, and dark-colored leaves are particularly abundant in polyphenolic compounds. Polyphenols have applications in folk medicine as antibiotic, anti-diarrheal, anti-ulcer, and anti-inflammatory agents. Several other diseases, for example, hypertension, have been successfully treated with plant extracts particularly rich in polyphenols. Researchers have identified more than 5,000 flavonoids (a form of polyphenol) in plants, some in fruits, beans, roots, and leaves, that are eaten as a food or used to make drinks. They are found in considerable quantities in fruit, fruit juices, vegetables, grains, tea, cocoa, red wine, and soy.

Chocolate

Scientists have known about the antioxidant activity of polyphenols in chocolate for over fifty years. These are responsible for the excellent keeping-qualities of chocolate and for preventing the dairy fats from becoming rancid. Now there is a growing body of evidence that cocoa flavonoids have cardiovascular health benefits, not only due to their antioxidant effects on LDL cholesterol, but also because of their aspirin-like effects on platelet function, their ability to relax the linings of arteries, their beneficial effects on immune function, and their anti-inflammatory role. The quantity of natural flavonoids in chocolate depends on the variety of cocoa bean, the growing conditions, processing, and storage.

Wine

In France, the incidence of heart disease is remarkably low, despite a diet rich in saturated fat and the presence of other risk factors (such as smoking and high cholesterol levels). This apparent contradiction has been termed "the French paradox" and has been attributed to the possibility that the French custom of drinking wine with meals may provide protection against heart disease.

The protective effects of moderate wine consumption are possibly due to the alcohol-induced increase in high-density lipoprotein (HDL) levels, and to the effects of the small amounts of polyphenols found in wine.

1 UNIT OF ALCOHOL IS:
1 glass of beer (10 fl. oz.)
1 small glass of red or white wine ($\frac{1}{2}$ cup/4 fl. oz.)
1 small measure of hard liquor (1 fl. oz.)
1 small glass of fortified wine, e.g., sherry, vermouth ($\frac{1}{4}$ cup/2 fl. oz.)

Drinking above sensible limits of alchohol, however, is a danger to health. It also supplies extra Calories (around 100 Calories per unit), which do not help if you have a weight problem. The Department of Health's current "sensible" daily limits suggest no more than two to three units (see table above) for women and three to four units for men. It is both the pattern of drinking and the amount that are important, rather than the type of drink. Avoid binge drinking and keep to safe levels of alcohol, with some alcohol-free days.

Key action points

- ▶ Keep to sensible drinking limits (see above) and quench thirst with water.
- ▶ Alternate alcoholic with non-alcoholic drinks.
- ▶ Drink at least 1½ quarts (6 8-oz glasses) of fluid each day, which can include tea, coffee, water, fruit juice, soft drinks, etc. (No more than six mugs of coffee are recommended because of the caffeine content.)

Olive oil

Olive oil is the principal source of fat in the Mediterranean diet. The flavor of extra virgin olive oil complements raw vegetables, which are generally dressed with olive oil and vinegar (the latter also contains antioxidants). Unlike other oils, olive oil contains phenolic compounds, which provide its unique aroma and taste, and have been shown to exert potent beneficial actions. Most vegetable oils are extracted from seeds by solvents, whereas olive oil is obtained from the whole fruit by means of physical pressure, without the use of chemicals. The phenolic fraction in extra virgin olive oil is significantly higher than in plain olive oil.

Antioxidant supplements

Recent clinical trials have confirmed that there seems little benefit in taking individual nutrients such as vitamins E, C, or betacarotene in supplement form. The advantages may occur only when the antioxidants are part of a cardioprotective diet in which the abundance of bioactive compounds provided by fruit, vegetables, wine, and olive oil work together to benefit your heart.

Folic acid

Fruit and vegetables also supply other protective nutrients such as folic acid. A diet with an adequate supply of folic acid, B6, and B12 vitamins helps to reduce the levels of homocysteine in the blood. Homocysteine is produced naturally in the body when protein is metabolized. High homocysteine levels have been associated with heart disease since high levels are toxic and can damage artery walls. Since 1998, the US Food and Drug Administration (FDA) has stipulated that enriched grain products, including breakfast cereals, be fortified with folic acid.

Concentrated sources of folic acid:
- liver
- yeast extract
- green leafy vegetables
- legumes
- oranges

Foods that have been fortified with folic acid, particularly breakfast cereals, are now widely available and can increase significantly total intake of folic acid.

Legumes

Legumes, such as beans and peas, and their dried seeds, are good sources of both insoluble fiber, and the cholesterol-lowering soluble fibre and are full of cardioprotective nutrients such as arginine, vitamin E, the B vitamins, folic acid, and minerals such as calcium, iron, and zinc. Vegetarians have been shown to have less risk of heart disease compared to non-vegetarians, and this is both because of their diet and also other healthy aspects of their lifestyles. Beans, peas and dried beans are low in fat and high in protein, and can be used instead of, or combined with, meat or fish. There is a great variety of beans to choose from: chickpeas, cranberry beans, lentils, black-eyed peas, peas, and corn. They can be bought dried, then soaked, and cooked in plenty of boiling water (usually for an hour or more) until soft. Lentils take a much shorter time to cook. Kidney beans release a toxic substance while they are being cooked, but as long as they are boiled rapidly for at least 10 minutes at the beginning of the cooking time, this substance is destroyed completely. There is also a great selection of canned beans which are just as nutritious, and available in most stores.

Soy beans

Soy beans are worth a separate mention since there is emerging evidence that increasing the amount of soy protein in the diet has health benefits for heart disease, cancer, women's health, and osteoporosis. Studies have shown that an intake of 25g per day of soy protein can reduce LDL cholesterol by about 10 percent. In the USA and UK, a health claim has been approved for soy which states that "25g of soy protein a day as part of a diet low in saturated fat and cholesterol may reduce the risk of heart disease."

It may be difficult to obtain 25g of soy protein per day, but some substitution of meat and dairy products is certainly possible. The soy bean contains some fat which is mainly polyunsaturated fat containing the essential fatty acids, linoleic and alpha-linolenic acid. Soy beans are a particularly useful source of the plant form of omega-3 fatty acids (alpha-linolenic acid). In addition to these nutrients, soybeans contain a wealth of phytochemicals. One potent group of phytochemicals called isoflavones is virtually unique to soy. Isoflavones are phytoestrogens with weak estrogenic effects, and Asian populations that regularly eat soy foods have a lower incidence of hormone-dependent cancers – breast, colon, and prostate cancers.

Traditional soy foods include soybeans, miso, soy milk, soybean oil, soy margarine, soy nuts, soy sauce, tempeh, tofu, and tofu products. New-generation soy products include concentrated forms of food ingredients such as soy protein isolate, soy protein concentrate, soy flour, and textured soy protein. Soy protein is typically consumed in the US as soy milk, yogurts, desserts, tofu, ground tofu and vegetarian sausages, and in a wide variety of bread and bakery products, e.g., cereal bars.

Nuts

Nuts are an important part of the cardioprotective diet. Recent studies suggest that frequent nut consumption may be protective against heart disease because of the beneficial effects on blood lipids. In clinical studies, diets supplemented with walnuts or almonds decreased levels of LDL cholesterol and total cholesterol. Other valuable constituents include high amounts of vegetable protein, magnesium, copper, vitamin E, folic acid, fiber, potassium, and alpha-linolenic acid (principally in

walnuts). Although nuts are high in fat, the fat is mostly unsaturated, which has positive effects on blood lipids. Most nuts are rich in arginine, the precursor of nitric oxide, which is important for the maintenance of a healthy lining in the arteries. Coconut is the exception, and contains a lot of saturated fat, particularly coconut cream, although coconut milk is lower in fat.

Seeds

Seeds are a valuable source of protein and essential fatty acids. Linseed (or flaxseed), sesame, pumpkin, and sunflower seeds are rich sources of the omega-3 fatty acids, while sesame and sunflower seeds also contain omega-6 fatty acids. All of these seeds are packed with a wealth of vitamins and minerals such as vitamins A, B, D, E, and K, and folic acid, as well as the minerals calcium, iron, magnesium, selenium, and zinc.

Plant sterols and stanols

Plant sterols are natural substances, the plant equivalents of cholesterol, and are found at low levels in foods that are rich in vegetable oils, such as sunflower oil, rapeseed oil (canola), soybean oil, and in cereals, nuts, and some vegetables. Stanols are largely derived from tall oil, a by-product of the pine industry. It has been known since the 1950s that sterols and stanols reduce the absorption of cholesterol in the body during digestion, but only recently have satisfactory methods for extracting, concentrating,

and adding them to various foods, such as spreads, soft cheese, yogurt, and cereal bars, been developed. Plant sterols and stanols lower cholesterol in the blood by reducing the absorption of cholesterol from the intestine. Clinical trials have shown that 2g of plant sterols, taken every day in spreads, will lower blood cholesterol by about 10 percent.

Key action points

▶ Try to eat a wide variety of fruit and vegetables. They can be fresh, frozen, or canned. Fruit juice counts, but only for one portion a day.

▶ Make the most of the enormous variety of beans, peas, and dried beans and seeds by infusing them with the flavors of olive oil, and vegetables such as onions, garlic, tomatoes, eggplants, and herbs.

▶ Try using soy milk, soy yogurts and desserts, traditional soy protein, such as tofu or miso, and textured soy protein, as low-fat, cholesterol-lowering alternatives to dairy foods and meat.

▶ Enjoy a variety of nuts and seeds in your cereals, salads, and main meals. These make truly nutritious snacks, especially when mixed with dried fruit; they are, however, a significant source of Calories, so beware if you are watching your weight!

▶ Mix seeds with garlic and herbs to make delicious dips. Tahini paste is an excellent creamy dip made from sesame seeds.

Whole-grain cereals, vegetables, and legumes in the cardioprotective diet

People in countries bordering the Mediterranean basin tend to consume a wide variety of starchy carbohydrate foods, from whole-grain cereals to vegetables and legumes. All types of bread, pasta, rice, oats, bulghur, tabbouleh, couscous, semolina, gnocchi, potatoes, and other fiber-rich vegetables such as legumes are the staple foods in this region. Starchy carbohydrates lend bulk and satisfying power to your food, making it filling but not fattening, as they contain only four Calories per gram.

Starchy carbohydrate foods and beans, peas and dried beans and seeds are the main source of fiber in the diet. Fiber is classed as both insoluble and soluble. Insoluble fiber, found in the outer layer of whole-grains and vegetables, is important for good bowel health. Soluble fiber is mainly found in beans, peas and dried beans and seeds, oats, barley, rye, and most fruits. It forms a gel-like mixture that slows down the digestion of foods, helping to regulate appetite and glucose levels, and lower blood cholesterol levels.

Whole-grains such as wheat, corn, oats, barley, rye, and rice also contain important cardioprotective nutrients including antioxidants, vitamins, and trace elements, namely vitamin E, B vitamins, zinc, and selenium.

Different carbohydrates affect the body in different ways, and this can be gauged by their "glycemic index" (GI). Foods with a lower glycemic index are better for heart health since they take longer to produce a rise in blood glucose, which ultimately improves the lipid profile by increasing HDL cholesterol.

Particularly low GI foods are:
- porridge, oats, and high-fiber breakfast cereals
- bread with added seeds and grains, rye, and pumpernickel
- pasta, noodles, basmati rice, new waxy potatoes, yams, and sweet potatoes
- beans, peas, and lentils
- traditional English stoned fruit (apples, pears, plums, peaches)
- oranges, bananas, and grapefruit

Key action points
- Breakfast cereals, including porridge oats, and granola, are a good way to start the day, and can be eaten as a healthy snack at any time.
- Base your meals and snacks around starchy carbohydrate foods by covering half of your dinner plate with potatoes, rice, or pasta, and accompanying them with a delicious variety of breads.
- Choose from the wide varieties of available breads, especially those with seeds and grains; there is no need to add spread.

- Whole-grain varieties of bread, cereals, pasta, and rice make healthy choices, taste better, and are also more satisfying.
- The chapati is bread at its simplest – just flour and water, with no added fat or salt.
- Potatoes eaten in their skins, or new potatoes in their skins, are filling, not fattening. Top baked potatoes with low-fat plain yogurt, fromage frais, or flavored cottage cheese rather than butter or margarine.

Moderate amounts of lean meat, fish, dairy foods, and eggs in the cardioprotective diet

The cardioprotective diet should contain moderate amounts of lean meat, fish, dairy foods, and eggs. "Mediterrasian" cuisine makes more use of beans, peas, and dried beans and seeds, either as vegetarian dishes or mixed with smaller quantities of meat or fish.

Small amounts of dairy foods are eaten in the cardioprotective diet. European cheeses and feta cheese are generally lower in fat, having higher water content,

TYPE OF CHEESE	PERCENTAGE FAT
Cottage cheese	4
Ricotta	11
Half-fat hard cheese	15
Feta	20
Mozzarella	21
Camembert	23
Edam	25
Brie	27
Soy	27
Emmental	30
Parmesan	33
Cheddar	34
Stilton	35

while skim milk products such as yogurt and fromage frais are a popular accompaniment to fresh fruit.

Eggs are eaten in moderation (see key action points, below). Although eggs contain a significant amount of dietary cholesterol in the yolk, it is the saturated fat content that actually increases blood cholesterol.

Key action points

▸ Eat moderate amounts of protein foods, but perhaps smaller than in the US traditional diet. Think of the meat or fish as more of a flavor accompaniment to your main meal of starchy carbohydrates, and vegetables or salad.

▸ If half your dinner plate is filled with starchy carbohydrates and two-thirds of the other half with vegetables or salad, then the final third should be for the protein part of your meal, whether fish or lean meat.

▸ Trim all visible fat from meat, and skin from poultry.

▸ Choose lower-fat dairy products such as skim or low-fat milk, lower-fat cheeses (see table, left), yogurt, and fromage frais.

▸ Keep to a moderate quantity of three to four eggs per week.

Salt and sugar in the cardioprotective diet

Salt or sodium chloride has been traditionally used mainly to preserve food. However, modern preservation methods have made it redundant, yet food manufacturers continue to supply processed foods packed with salt because we have become accustomed to the taste. Excessive salt consumption causes a significant rise in blood pressure, which is a major cause of stroke and heart attacks. Government recommendations are to decrease our salt intake by half, to six grams per day (just one teaspoonful). Average blood pressure has fallen in countries which have launched public awareness campaigns to decrease salt intake, and where potassium chloride is used in baked and processed foods.

As well as decreasing sodium, increasing potassium seems to be important in decreasing blood pressure. Potassium is found in abundant quantities in fruits and vegetables.

We are also born with a sweet tooth and while sugar intake is not directly associated with heart disease, sweet foods can add unwanted calories to the diet and may also contain saturated fat. In a cardioprotective diet, natural sweetness is provided by sumptuous fruits of all kinds, fresh, canned and dried, all with the added bonus of providing antioxidants, vitamins, and minerals such as potassium.

Key action points

▸ Avoid adding salt to your cooking and to your food at the table. Rather enhance the natural flavors of your dishes with aromatic vegetables, herbs, and spices such as garlic, onions, pepper, lemon juice, vinegar, ginger, chiles, and tomatoes.

▶ Steaming and microwaving vegetables are the best ways to cook vegetables to retain all their top nutrients, flavor and taste. Serve as soon as they are cooked.

▶ Use fresh foods wherever possible and avoid processed foods. A huge amount of our salt intake (75 percent) comes from processed foods.

▶ Check the label for the sodium content of processed foods and choose foods which contain less than 0.1g or 100mg per serving for main meals and 0.1g or 100mg per 100g for snacks.

▶ If you want to know the amount of salt (sodium chloride) in a product, multiply the sodium by 2.5. For example, 1g of sodium per 100g = 2.5g of salt per 100g.

▶ Try to keep your daily sodium intake to below 2.5g (2,500mg) of sodium (or 6.25g of salt). In practice, this is hard to do since most of your daily intake comes from processed foods.

▶ Remember: some foods that do not appear to be salty, such as bread and some cereals, can contain large quantities of salt. Check the labels.

▶ Kosher salt and sea salt are still salt, and should be avoided. You could use a salt substitute which contains less sodium, to wean yourself off the salt habit.

▶ Stocks and gravies can be made from salt-free, homemade ingredients, and you can purée vegetables such as onions, garlic, tomatoes, and eggplants with a little wine, to make sauces. For speed, "diluted" stocks and gravies can be made by using half the usual quantities of bouillon cubes or gravy granules.

▶ Look for vegetables, fish, and beans canned in water rather than brine, and choose lower-salt varieties of baked beans, bread, yeast extract, bouillon, ketchup and soy sauce.

▶ Feed your sweet tooth with natural sweetness from fresh, canned, frozen, or dried fruit.

▶ Look for low-sugar varieties of sodas, jams and marmalades, jello, baked beans, tomato sauces, and fruit canned in natural juices.

▶ Salty and sugary solutions can be removed from canned produce by rinsing in a colander under the tap.

A Whole Lifestyle Approach

Healthy Eating for Your Heart is just one part of a complementary lifestyle approach towards better health – to help you get in shape, feel fitter, and have more energy. You can make it easy for yourself by making changes gradually, rather than all at once. You'll be surprised by how even the smallest of changes can make a difference.

When it comes to eating, a balanced approach is best: there are no good or bad foods, and you can still enjoy the odd indulgence occasionally, guilt-free, provided that for the majority of time you eat:

- plenty of fruit and vegetables including legumes, nuts, and seeds
- plenty of bread and other cereals (like pasta, rice) and potatoes
- moderate amounts of milk and dairy foods, low-fat where possible
- moderate amounts of lean meat and fish
- small amounts of fatty and sugary foods

Not smoking and engaging in plenty of physical activity are also part of this lifestyle package. If you enjoy keeping active and follow the key messages above, you will manage your weight and feel all the better for being in control.

Weight management
Energy taken "in" from the food we eat each day should equal the energy we expend "out" in the energy needs of our body and in our daily physical activity. If our "energy in" is greater than our "energy out", this will result in weight gain. Our energy balance is so fine that it only takes an extra cookie each day to gain four and a half pounds in a year! We also have to eat 3,500 calories less to lose a pound, and that is why losing weight is so difficult. It is much better to lose weight slowly – one to two pounds per week – and maintain the weight loss, than to do crash dieting only to regain the weight quickly, then have to diet again. Following the healthy lifestyle advice in this book will help you to make the changes necessary to control your weight for good, by eating a cardioprotective diet and taking more physical activity.

Feeding the family
We all want to give our children the best possible start in life. Making the best food choices for our children helps them to form good eating habits and attitudes to food that will influence their tastes and well-being far into the future.

Key action points
- Get your children involved with choosing, planning, and preparing meals, and in shopping.
- Hands-on cooking with children encourages a love of food, and cooking and can be fun, too.
- Just cook one meal for the whole family which you can enjoy eating all together.

- Always serve vegetables, bread, and water with your meal.
- Keep the fruit bowl well stocked with a variety of fresh produce, to eat whenever you feel those hunger pangs start.
- Try new foods with old favorites.

Adapting traditional family recipes
- Reduce the amount of fat used.
- Change the type of fat by using a monounsaturated or polyunsaturated variety.
- Cut out the salt.
- Reduce the amount of meat and add more legumes.
- Replace pie dough in pies with mashed potatoes to top them instead, e.g., shepherd's pie.
- Reduce the amount of sugar used; sweeten instead with dried fruit or fruit juice.
- Use yogurt or fromage frais instead of cream.
- Use half-fat cheese or smaller quantities of stronger cheeses, e.g., Parmesan.
- Grating cheese makes it go further.
- Instead of high-fat roux-based sauces, make sauces with cornstarch and skim milk; flavor with mustard and black pepper.

Remember: forming good eating habits is just part of a lifestyle package, and encouraging children to be more active and exercise regularly, and not to smoke is equally important.

A cardioprotective kitchen

A kitchen with the following equipment will encourage healthy cooking:

- Good-quality, heavy, non-stick pans make low-fat cooking easier as they allow food to be cooked more efficiently without fat.
- Ridged grill pans and special low-fat grills allow fat to drain away from meat and meat products.
- In summer, low-fat cooking is simple with a barbecue. In winter, stews, casseroles, and one-pot cooking encourage healthy infusions of cardioprotective nutrients.
- Microwaving and steaming food are the best ways to retain the maximum amount of nutrients.
- A non-stick wok is useful for low-fat stir-frying using a little oil, stock, or wine.
- An oil-water spray allows successful low-fat frying whether you are using a frying pan, ridged grill pan or roasting in the oven. The spray can be used directly on cooking equipment, or the food itself may be given the lightest possible spray, to stop it from drying out during cooking, or from sticking to the pan. Oil-water sprays can be bought commercially or made up at home by combining your favorite high-quality oils (add seven parts water to one part oil). Use rapeseed oil (canola) for general purposes, olive oil for a richer flavor, walnut oil for a piquant fragrance, and sesame oil for oriental dishes. Oils can be flavor-infused with your favorite herbs and spices for added zest.

Check the labels

In the real world, it is not always possible to cook from scratch, and there will be times when you will need to buy pre-prepared foods or ingredients for your meal. By checking the information on a food label, you will be able to make healthy choices by choosing foods which are low in fat, low in saturated fat, high in fiber, and low in sugar and salt.

Ingredients are generally listed on labels in decreasing order by weight. You can also use the nutritional information and the table on page 34 to see if the product contains a lot of or a little fat, saturated fat, fiber, sugar, or sodium.

For ready-meals and other foods eaten in large amounts as a main meal, look at the amount per serving. Check the serving size with the amount you usually eat! For snacks and other foods eaten in smaller amounts, look at the "per serving" information. You can also use this information to compare products and choose the healthiest option.

The nutritional information on a "ready meal" beef lasagne is shown in the table below. The suggested serving size for this lasagne is 400g and you can see that it contains "a lot" of fat, saturated fat, sugars, and salt (see the table on page 34) and would not be a healthy choice.

Guideline daily amounts

You may also use the figures on a package to help you work out how the food fits into your whole diet for that

Nutritional information from a package of beef lasagne

TYPICAL COMPOSITION	THIS PACK (400G) PROVIDES	100G (3½OZ) PROVIDES
Energy	2304kJ/548kcals	576kJ/137kcals
Protein	34.4g	8.6g
Carbohydrate	47.2g	11.8g
of which sugars	12.8g	3.2g
Fat	24.8g	6.2g
of which saturates	14.8g	3.7g
Sodium	1.6g	0.4g

A serving (400g/14 oz.) contains the equivalent of approximately 4g of salt

Nutritional guidelines

A LOT	A LITTLE
20g fat	3g fat
5g saturates	1g saturates
3g fiber	0.5g fibre
10g sugars	2g sugars
0.5g sodium	0.1g sodium

If you want to know the amount of salt (sodium chloride) in a product, multiply the sodium by 2.5.

day. The figures in the table below are based on an average-sized man or woman engaging in an average amount of physical activity.

The beef lasagne, therefore, for a man, contains about a quarter of the recommended amount of fat for the day, and half the recommended amount

Guideline daily amounts

	MEN	WOMEN
Energy	2,500 Calories	2,000 Calories
Fat	95g	70g
Saturates	30g	20g
Fibre	20g	16g
Sugar	70g	50g
Sodium	2.5g	2g

of saturated fat. This means that your food for the rest of the day must be particularly low in fat and saturated fat to keep within healthy guidelines.

Claims

Choose foods that have general claims:
- healthy eating
- diet, reduced calorie, or low-calorie
- low-fat (should have no more than 5g of fat per 100g)
- reduced fat or virtually fat-free
- low-salt or reduced salt
- sugar-free

but at the same time beware:
- Low-fat or fat-free does not necessarily mean low-calorie or calorie-free since the food may be full of sugar and as high in calories as the standard product.
- Cholesterol-free foods may be full of fat and calories.
- Sugar-free does not mean low-calorie or low-fat; such foods may be high in both.

Eating out

Inevitably, we can't always eat at home. In fact some of us eat "out" almost as much as we eat at home, whether it's socially, a lunch-time sandwich, "bites" after work, or celebration meals. Healthy eating can present a challenge at these times but needn't be a nightmare. If you only go out occasionally, don't worry – just enjoy your treat! If you do eat out a lot, then you will need to use your knowledge to make healthy choices from the menu. After a

while, you will learn to return to the restaurant where you know that it is easy to choose the food you prefer to eat, and where the food is delicious and healthy too!

Key action points in restaurants
- Take some plain bread from the bread basket but decline the butter. Ask for extra bread and try different varieties.
- Simple appetizers include chilled fruit juice, melon cocktail, salads with a little olive oil dressing. Choose a vegetable-based soup with a crusty bread roll.
- Choose a baked potato (no butter) with a variety of fillings. Don't forget the side salad!
- Choose plenty of vegetables or a side salad with your main course. Avoid salads with mayonnaise-based dressings; ask for a little olive oil, vinegar, or oil-free dressing instead.
- Go for dishes which are steamed, braised, broiled, char-grilled, or baked.
- Vegetarian options based around beans and legumes with pasta, rice, potatoes, bread, and extra vegetables and salads make good choices.
- Water is a good thirst-quencher and appetite-queller, so always ask for a pitcher with your meal.
- For a dessert, choose fresh fruit salad or just fresh fruit. Sherberts, low-fat frozen yogurts, or ice milks, if available, make for a less-guilty option.

In Italian restaurants

▶ Go for bread sticks or plain crusty bread, and avoid garlic bread.

▶ Choose thin-crust pizza with vegetable toppings, ham, chicken, tuna, and seafood. These pizzas tend to be the least calorific and least fatty.

▶ Choose pasta with tomato-based or seafood sauces, e.g., arrabbiata sauce, napoletana, vongole, primavera, provençale, puttanesca, and so on. Avoid creamy sauces.

▶ Traditional Italian dishes such as lasagne and spaghetti bolognese can be very high in fat. Some lasagnes contain more fat than a plate of fish and chips! Choose cannelloni instead, since the spinach replaces some of the fatty meat.

In Indian restaurants

▶ Choose drier curries such as tandoori and tikka dishes.

▶ Choose saffron rice or plain boiled rice.

▶ Choose plain chapatis or nan breads. Ghee, the Indian cooking fat, is similar to butter in its saturated fat content, so it should be avoided.

▶ Add generous amounts of vegetables to all curry dishes. In an Indian or Pakistani home, a meat curry is seldom eaten on its own.

▶ Choose tomato-based sauces like lamb rogan josh and chicken jalfrezi.

▶ Vegetable, chicken, and shrimp Madras are suitable, as are Balti or dupiaza dishes.

▶ Avoid creamy dishes such as korma, passandra, and masala, and oily dishes such as Bhajis, samosas, or pakoras.

In Chinese restaurants

▶ Choose soups for appetizers rather than battered egg rolls.

▶ "Stewed" dishes, e.g., chicken with bean sprouts or pineapple, chile shrimp or crab, are good choices.

▶ Chow mein or boiled, steamed rice are good starchy bases for your meal.

▶ Stir-fried dishes are lower in fat than deep-fried dishes.

▶ Avoid deep-fried foods such as shrimp chips and sweet 'n' sour balls.

In Thai restaurants

▶ For appetizers, clear soups, seafood salads, and stir-fried dishes are suitable. Avoid the deep-fried options.

▶ Choose steamed or "sticky" rice.

▶ Avoid dishes with coconut cream.

In Mexican restaurants

▶ Good appetizer choices are spicy corn chowder and black bean soup.

▶ Fill up on Mexican rice and vegetable chili.

▶ Fajitas and soft tortilla wraps are a good bet, but beware of high-fat enchiladas!

▶ Guacamole and refried beans are a mixed bag, as they contain a lot of cardioprotective nutrients but are also high in fat, so take it easy!

▶ Watch out for sour cream, tortilla chips, cheese, deep-fried tortillas!

Fast foods

▶ In the burger bar, choose a plain hamburger, cheeseburger, or grilled chicken burger, and order the smallest size. Share any fries and choose water, fruit juice, or a diet drink.

▶ Choose a falafel sandwich or shish kabob.

▶ Opt for broiled fish and chicken and avoid batter-coated ones. Share any fries, and add some vegetables.

Key action points with snacks

▶ When eating sandwiches, good fillings are tuna, salmon, sardines, pilchards, roast lean meat, ham, chicken, turkey, egg, Edam, Brie, low-fat cream cheese, hummus, peanut butter, and salads.

▶ Choose "diet", "light" and "healthy option" sandwiches. Avoid mayonnaise, and look for moist alternatives such as mustard, pickles, and yogurt or fromage frais.

▶ Fresh fruits and fruit salads, or a handful of fresh nuts and dried fruits are good snacks.

▶ Yogurts and rice puddings – choose low-fat or "light" varieties.

▶ Fruit buns, fruit scones, malt bread, crumpets, and large pretzels make filling snacks.

▶ Ginger snaps, golden fruit raisin biscuits, and fig rolls are good low-fat choices.

A Chef's Prescription

During the early years of my training, I soon learned that "where there is fat, there is flavor", and if I am honest with myself, I have to agree – fat tastes good. And while there are obvious health problems associated with too much fat, simply omitting it from a dish without compensation will cause a meal to be a bland and uninteresting experience – a non-event, in fact. So the question we need to ask ourselves is how to remove the fat without sacrificing the taste.

Not so long ago, the notion of healthy eating implied denial, deprivation and boring food. But the great chefs such as Anton Mosimann in Britain and Michel Guérard in France have pioneered healthy, low-fat food, teaching us to cook without too much fat, cream, and butter. With a little thought, it is actually very easy to do just this – without creating "rabbit food".

Let me say from the outset that this cookbook is not part of a fad. It is a book about healthy eating in today's world, using only the best-quality ingredients with imagination, flair, and thought. In this book I draw on the 30 years I have spent in professional kitchens, and the eclectic tastes that I have encountered while traveling the world. From these experiences, I have devised over 100 recipes, presented with love and care, while meeting all the nutritional guidelines. Some of the recipes are gourmet, some are more everyday in design, and there is something for every taste. This book will teach you to eat smart, heart smart, but above all, that you don't have to choose between good food and good health.

Healthy Low-fat Cooking Methods

Kitchen equipment

You can prepare great-tasting, healthy meals with basic cooking pots and pans, and utensils, but I would recommend that you buy a few well-made pieces that will make cooking easier and help you to obtain the most successful results:

- heavy, non-stick, frying pan
- heavy, non-stick, deep-sided frying pan, suitable for oven use
- heavy, non-stick, casserole dish with lid
- non-stick roasting pan
- non-stick baking tray

Grilling and broiling

This is an extremely healthy way to prepare food and is ideal for cooking low-fat food, since you only need to spray the smallest amount of oil over your meat, fish (none is needed on oily fish), or vegetables to prevent them from sticking. Use a broiler rack under a conventional broiler, or a preheated grill pan, and remember to take advantage of the summer months by cooking on an open-grill or barbecue.

Baking

Another low-fat cooking method. I prefer to bake small pieces of meat or fish in a non-stick baking dish. Alternatively, you can bake them in a sealed foil pouch with some fresh herbs or spices, and stock. This method is very grandly known as cooking *en papillote*, but is very simple to do. The resultant juices, collected in the foil, can then be used to create an accompanying sauce.

Roasting

This is not usually associated with healthy cooking as the roasting meats are usually larger in size and fattier in composition. Buy the leanest meat available. It is also better to roast small cuts of meat and seal them first in a frying pan, along with a very small amount of oil. If you are roasting a large piece of meat, cook it on a wire rack so that the fat drains away during cooking. A good tip is to add a few ice cubes to the baking dish; the water will help the fat solidify, which can then be removed with a spoon or paper towels.

Steaming

This is perhaps the most nutritious cooking method and it requires no added fat. Instead it uses the vapor created by boiling water or stock to cook the vegetables, fish, or meat that is stacked above the liquid. A simple collapsible steamer that fits snugly inside a saucepan, topped with a tight-fitting lid, is all you need for this, or you could rest a colander on top of a saucepan and cover it with foil. Chinese bamboo steamers are becoming more popular, and you can stack several layers on top of each other, which will let you to cook more than one food at once.

Slow-poaching and boiling

Again, these require no additional oil. Any fat released by poaching foods can be removed using paper towels. Poached foods are also generally easy to digest.

Braising

This involves cooking meat, fish, or vegetables in a flavored liquid in an ovenproof dish. Generally, the food is first seared in butter or oil before being immersed in stock, but this is not essential. Dry-fry meat (or use a minimal amount of oil) in a non-stick pan until the meat is slightly colored all over, before transferring to the casserole dish. Vegetables are often added at this stage, along with any herbs or spices, and then the dish is oven-cooked (unless you have a flameproof dish suitable for stove use).

Microwaving

Those of you who have read my previous books will know that I am not usually a fan of the microwave. However, through

my research for this book, I have learned to be more tolerant and must admit that it does have a useful role in low-fat cooking. Microwave cooking rarely needs any fat, and it is also particularly good for cooking vegetables since it needs only a small amount of liquid to cook them, thus retaining all the nutrients as well as texture and color.

Stir-frying

This is synonymous with Oriental food, and a method that we have come to enjoy. It is also a quick and nutritious way to cook, using little or no oil. The ingredients cook rapidly in a wok, retaining the crunchiness of the vegetables and the juiciness of meat and fish.

Dry-frying

This seals meat or fish in a very hot, non-stick pan without using any fat, and is perfect for starting casseroles or meat sauces such as the classic bolognese sauce. Dry-frying browns the meat evenly and the fat leaks out of the meat as it cooks, so you can drain it away easily. If you must add some fat, use an oil/water cooking spray (see page 33).

Vaporized frying

Here, chopped vegetables are sautéed in a non-stick pan or wok with a small amount of water or stock instead of oil. The liquid evaporates, coaxing the vegetables to release their natural flavors and caramelize slightly. An excellent way to exude flavor without using fat.

Chef's Tips

▶ Casseroles that combine meat, vegetables, and legumes or grains make tasty, filling meals.

▶ Herbs and spices produce intense flavor to compensate for the lack of fat. Dried herbs are fine to use, but their aroma and taste cannot be compared with those of fresh herbs. Ideally, fresh spices should be toasted to maximize flavor before adding to dishes. Fresh herbs should be added at the last minute for most effect.

▶ Marinating meat and fish in low-fat yogurt, spices, herbs, flavored vinegars, and Asian-style sauces such as teriyaki or sweet chile sauce, will add moisture, tenderize it, and give it flavour.

▶ Make your own low-fat stocks and sauces, and freeze the left-overs for future use. You can also use the left-over liquid from cooking vegetables.

▶ When making soups, stews, and casseroles, skim the fat that rises to the surface while cooking. A good idea is to make them a day ahead, then store in the fridge overnight. Any fat in the dish will rise to the surface as it cools, and can easily be removed once it has solidified. This type of dish actually improves in flavor when cooked in advance.

▶ Use egg whites as a binding for stuffings or when making crumb coating since it contains no fat. As a general rule, in a recipe, replace one whole egg with two egg whites.

▶ If used for cooking purposes, low-fat spreads must contain a minimum of 40 percent fat.

▶ Take great care when cooking with no-fat or low-fat dairy products such as yogurt and low-fat cheeses since they can curdle when boiled. Let them come to room temperature first, then add them as needed to the dish while removed from the heat. Skim milk can be boiled but can separate when combined with acidic juices from lemons or tomatoes.

▶ Replace the cream in cream-based dished with skim milk, and thicken the sauce with cornstarch or flour, adding a spoonful of low-fat unflavored fromage frais or yogurt before serving.

▶ One of my favorite additions to dishes is roasted garlic purée and I always keep a batch handy. Simply place unpeeled garlic cloves in a microwave and cook for six to eight minutes on full power until they soften. Let cool before popping them out of their skins, and crush with a mortar and pestle, or blend to a smooth purée. Store in an airtight container.

Simple Low-fat Stocks

It is simple to make your own stocks, and these recipes can be prepared up to four days ahead and stored, covered, in the fridge. Be sure to remove any fat from the surface after the cooled stock has been refrigerated overnight. If the stock is to be kept longer, it is best to freeze it in smaller quantities. Prepared stocks are also now available in supermarkets, but be aware of their salt content. Bouillon cubes or powder can also be used. As a guide, one small crumbled bouillon cube mixed with two and a half cups (20 fl. oz.) water will give a fairly strong stock. However, check the salt content of bouillon cubes and powders.

All low-fat stocks, per 2½ cups (18 fl. oz.):
14 Calories, 0.2g fat, 0g saturated fat,
0.65g sodium

Beef stock

4½ pounds meaty beef bones
2 medium onions, chopped
2 stalks celery, chopped
2 medium carrots, chopped
1 bay leaf
2 teaspoons black peppercorns
5¼ quarts water

Place the bones and onions in a baking dish. Bake in a hot oven for one hour or until the bones and onions are well browned. Transfer the bones and onions to a large pot, then add the celery, carrots, bay leaf, peppercorns, and water. Simmer, uncovered, for three hours, then strain. Makes about two and a half quarts.

Chicken stock

4½ pounds chicken bones
2 medium onions, chopped
2 stalks celery, chopped
2 medium carrots, chopped
1 bay leaf
2 teaspoons black peppercorns
5¼ quarts water

Combine all the ingredients in a large pot. Simmer, uncovered for two hours, then strain. Makes two and a half quarts.

Fish stock

3¼ pounds fish bones
3 quarts water
1 medium onion, chopped
2 stalks celery, chopped
1 bay leaf
1 teaspoon black peppercorns

Combine all the ingredients in a large pan. Simmer, uncovered, for 20 minutes, then strain. Makes two and a half quarts.

Vegetable stock

1 large carrot, chopped
1 large parsnip, chopped
2 medium onions, chopped
6 stalks celery, chopped
1 bay leaf
2 teaspoons black peppercorns
3 quarts water

Combine all the ingredients in a large pot. Simmer, uncovered, for one hour, then strain. Makes about five and a quarter cups.

Breakfasts and Brunches

1

Fragrant fruit compote
As a chef, I find the standard fruit compote somewhat boring, so I decided to give my recipe a little Middle Eastern flair with the addition of some fragrant sweet spices and flavorings instead of the more traditional sugar syrup. **Serves** 4

Juice and peel of 1 orange
1 teaspoon ground cinnamon
2 cloves
2 tablespoons orange blossom honey
¼ cup golden raisins
11 ounces selection of ready to eat dried fruits (apricots, prunes, figs) —about 1¾-2 cups

1 tablespoon orange flower water
Juice of ½ lemon
⅓ cup blanched almonds
⅓ cup pine nuts

Place the orange juice, peel, cinnamon, and cloves in a pan, with two-thirds cup water, and bring to a boil. Add the honey and raisins, and poach for two to three minutes.

Cut the dried fruits into bite-size pieces and add to the pan. Cook for one minute further, then remove from the heat. Let cool, then place in the fridge overnight.

One hour before serving, add the orange flower water and lemon juice. Let stand at room temperature to allow the flavors to meld together.

Divide the fruits into four serving bowls, scatter the almonds and pine nuts on top, and serve.

Per serving: 320 Calories, 13g fat, 1g saturated fat, 0.03g sodium

Breakfast sundae
Take a few exotic fruits, vibrant with flavor and color, and you have a refreshing breakfast sundae, which will instantly provide a good proportion of your recommended daily fruit amount. Almonds will also help to reduce your cholesterol levels. **Serves** 4

1 mango, peeled, and cut into ½-inch chunks
1 papaya, peeled, cut in half, and seeds removed
2 kiwi fruits, peeled, and cut into ½-inch chunks
1 banana, peeled, and thickly sliced
1 heaped cup strawberries, cut in half

Juice and peel of 1 orange
1 tablespoon mint leaves, roughly chopped
4 scoops of ricotta sorbet (see page 154)
⅔ cup low-fat plain yogurt
2 passion fruits, cut in half
2 tablespoons slivered almonds, toasted

Place all the fruits except the passion fruit in a bowl, add the orange juice, orange peel and mint leaves, and leave for 30 minutes in the fridge.

To serve, place a scoop of ricotta sorbet in four individual sundae-style glasses. Top with the fruits, then spoon the yogurt over the top. Scoop out the passion fruit pulp and seeds, and drizzle that on top.

Sprinkle a few almonds over the yogurt, and serve immediately.

Per serving: 306 Calories, 8g fat, 3g saturated fat, 0.08g sodium

Hot buttermilk crumpets with red and black fruits

Crumpets are light and delicious when made with buttermilk (you could use ordinary skim milk if you can't get the buttermilk, or try mixing ½ cup low-fat yogurt with 1 cup skim milk). **Serves 4**

4 cups all-purpose flour
Pinch of salt
2½ cups buttermilk (or skim milk)
1 tablespoon (½ oz) fresh yeast
Large pinch of baking soda
¼ cup warm water
Oil-water spray (see page 33)
Peel of 1 lemon

Low-fat plain yogurt, for serving (optional)
For the fruits
3 tablespoons sugar
2 cups mixed soft berries (strawberries, raspberries, blackberries, blueberries)
2 tablespoons honey
Juice of 1 lemon

Place the flour and salt in a large bowl and make a well in the center. Heat the buttermilk until it is tepid, add the yeast and dissolve, then pour into the well.

Use your hands to combine the mixture together into a batter. Cover with a cloth and leave in a warm place for about one hour until the mixture has risen. Mix the baking soda with the warm water and beat into the batter. Leave for another hour. Add the lemon peel and leave for a further 10 minutes.

Warm a non-stick frying pan over low heat, then squirt with a little oil-water spray. Place some shallow metal rings or cookie cutters in the pan.

Pour some of the batter into the rings to about a half-inch deep, and cook over low heat until a small indentation appears on the surface of the batter. Turn them over and continue cooking for a further couple of minutes. Cook seven more crumpets in this way, and keep warm.

For the fruits, place the sugar in a pan with three tablespoons water, and bring to a boil slowly. Add the fruits and cook for one minute, then add the honey and lemon juice and let cool slightly.

Serve the crumpets topped with the fruits, and with some low-fat yogurt, if you like.

Per serving: 522 Calories, 3g fat, 1g saturated fat, 0.47g sodium

Summer fruit crisp
When it comes to breakfast, I've always been able to kick-start the day on nothing more than a large cup of coffee. However, occasionally I enjoy the fresh taste of a fruity breakfast, so here is my "breakfast crumble," ripe fruits with a crisp granola topping that really hits the spot. **Serves 4**

2 ripe peaches
²⁄₃ cup raspberries
1 mango
1 cup blueberries
1 cup strawberries, cut in half
1 tablespoon lemon juice
½ teaspoon ground cinnamon
Good-quality raspberry jam

½ cup virtually fat-free fromage frais, or yogurt, for serving

For the topping
¾ cup granola
5 tablespoons wholewheat flour
2 tablespoons brown sugar
2 tablespoons low-fat spread

Preheat the oven to 425°F.

Blanch the peaches in boiling water for one minute, remove with a slotted spoon, and quickly refresh in cold water. Peel the peaches and cut in half, remove the pit, and cut into thick slices.

Place all the fruits in a bowl and mix with the lemon juice and cinnamon. Arrange the fruits attractively in four individual ovenproof dishes.

To make the topping, combine all the ingredients together in a bowl.

Sprinkle the topping over the fruits evenly. Bake in the oven for five to six minutes or until the topping is golden and crispy, then remove.

Meanwhile, heat the jam with two tablespoons water until it liquefies. Drizzle it over the topping and serve warm with a good dollop of fromage frais or yogurt.

Per serving: 301 Calories, 5g fat, 1g saturated fat, 0.16g sodium

Wheat germ muesli
Mix grain, nuts, and sweet poached fruits in a bowl and lace with honey for a wholesome start to the day. Wheat germ contains vitamin B and is often used as a dietary supplement. It is widely available from health food stores. **Serves 4**

1 cup organic wheat germ
1¼ cups apple juice
2 Granny Smith apples, peeled, cored, and grated
1 cup low-fat natural yogurt
1 cup mixed nuts (almonds, cashews, hazelnuts, macadamias), coarsely chopped

¼ cup honey
2 tablespoons lemon juice
²⁄₃ cup poached fruits (pears, apricots, prunes)

Place the wheat germ in a bowl, pour in the apple juice, then cover with a cloth and let soak overnight at room temperature.

Next day, add the apples, yogurt, nuts, half the honey, and the lemon juice, and stir well together.

Spoon into four serving bowls, top with a selection of poached fruits, and then drizzle the remaining honey on top to serve.

Per serving: 438 Calories, 19g fat, 1g saturated fat, 0.06g sodium

Banana and cinnamon pancakes with maple-raisin syrup

A real treat for breakfast lovers everywhere, this is perfect for lazy breakfasts and late brunches. Choose soy milk instead of semi-skim for a really nutritious option. **Serves 4**

1¼ cups self-rising flour	4 medium bananas
¼ cup soft brown sugar	½ cup maple syrup
1½ teaspoons ground cinnamon	3 tablespoons raisins, soaked until swollen in warm water, then drained
½ cup soy milk or semi-skim milk	2 tablespoons confectioners' sugar
1 egg yolk	
2 egg whites	

Place the flour in a bowl and add the sugar, cinnamon, milk, and egg yolk. Whisk until thoroughly combined. In a separate bowl, beat the egg whites until they form soft peaks, then gently fold them into the yolk mixture.

Heat a small non-stick frying pan or omelette pan. Pour approximately a quarter-cup batter at a time gently into the center of the pan, and tilt the pan to ensure even coating of the bottom. Cook over medium heat until golden brown on both sides, flipping over once during the cooking. Prepare seven more pancakes in this way and keep warm.

Peel the bananas and cut into thick slices. Heat the syrup and raisins in a small pan and, when boiling rapidly, add the bananas along with two tablespoons water. Continue cooking over high heat until the bananas are golden and caramelized, this will take about two to three minutes.

Divide the pancakes on to four serving plates and dust liberally with the confectioners' sugar. Top with the caramelized bananas, and drizzle any remaining raisin syrup on top, to serve.

Per serving: 428 Calories, 3g fat, 1g saturated fat, 0.19g sodium

Oatmeal mustard herrings

Herring is a wonderful fish — full of flavor and packed with natural goodness — yet ignored by many with the exception, perhaps, of the Scandinavians, who find terrific ways to serve it. Here is my favorite version, using flavors a little closer to home. **Serves 4**

	For the caper tartare
4 medium (4½ oz.) herrings, filleted	¼ cup reduced-calorie mayonnaise
Freshly ground black pepper	¼ cup low-fat plain yogurt
1 tablespoon prepared English mustard	2 tablespoons superfine capers, rinsed and chopped
1 heaped cup fresh white bread crumbs	2 tablespoons flat-leaf parsley, roughly chopped
1 cup fine oatmeal	Squeeze of lemon juice
Oil-water spray (see page 33)	
1 lemon, cut into wedges	

Preheat the broiler to its highest setting.

Using a small knife, lightly score the herring fillets on each side, being careful not to score them through. Season with black pepper to taste, and brush liberally with the mustard.

Mix the breadcrumbs and oatmeal together in a bowl, then liberally sprinkle them over the herrings, ensuring a good even coating. Turn the fillets over carefully and coat the other side well.

Lightly spray a baking tray with the oil-water spray. Place the herring fillets on the tray and broil for two to three minutes on each side.

Meanwhile, prepare the tartare sauce. Mix the mayonnaise and yogurt in a bowl along with the capers and parsley. Add the lemon juice and season to taste.

Serve the broiled herrings with the lemon wedges and a good dollop of caper tartare on the side.

Per serving: 399 Calories, 22g fat, 4g saturated fat, 0.52g sodium

Open-faced smoked salmon tortilla

Here the tortillas form the base of a pizza. This recipe is very tasty, and the ideal way to use up any scraps of lox (smoked salmon) you may have left over. Flour tortillas freeze very well and so make ideal pizza bases at a moment's notice. **Serves 4**

1 teaspoon unsaturated oil
1 small onion, finely chopped
14½-ounce can tomatoes, chopped
1 tablespoon tomato paste
2 canned anchovy fillets, drained and finely chopped
Freshly ground black pepper
Four 8-inch soft wheat flour tortillas

14 ounces lox (smoked salmon), roughly chopped
2 scallions, shredded
2 tablespoons fresh dill, roughly chopped, plus some to garnish
1 ounce half-fat mozzarella cheese, coarsely grated (about 2-3 tablespoons)

Preheat the oven to 425°F.

In a small pan, heat the oil, then add the onion and cook for two minutes over medium heat until softened. Add the tomatoes, tomato paste, and anchovies, and cook for six to eight minutes or until the mixture thickens to a pulpy consistency. Season with black pepper to taste.

Spread the tomato mix evenly over the four flour tortillas, scatter the lox on top, followed by the scallions and chopped dill.

Scatter the mozzarella over the top, place on a large baking tray, and cook for three to five minutes or until the cheese has melted.

Sprinkle the dill over the top, cut each tortilla into four equal wedges, and serve.

Per serving: 340 Calories, 10g fat, 2g saturated fat, 2.59g sodium

Raspberry and orange muffins

People have long had a passion for pancakes, muffins, and biscuits; they love them at any time of the day. I've never really understood until recently how good they can be for breakfast and mid-morning snacks. **Makes 12**

2½ cups all-purpose flour, sifted
1 tablespoon baking powder, sifted
½ cup sugar
1 tablespoon grated orange peel

1 large egg
1 cup buttermilk
¼ cup unsaturated oil
1 cup fresh or frozen raspberries

Preheat the oven to 400°F.

Place the flour and baking powder in a bowl. Add the sugar and orange peel, mix well, then make a well in the center.

Mix the egg and buttermilk with the oil in a separate bowl, then pour into the well in the flour, and mix. Add the raspberries and gently fold into the mixture.

Fill a 12-compartment, deep, muffin pan with 12 paper muffin cups. Spoon the mixture into the paper muffin cups.

Bake in the oven for 25 minutes until golden brown. Let cool before eating them.

Per serving (1 muffin): 166 Calories, 5g fat, 0g saturated fat, 0.17g sodium

Mango coconut porridge with jaggery (palm sugar)

This unusual porridge is creamy and will have you coming back for more. The mango gives the sugar and coconut milk a fragrant fruity balance. For the best porridge, soak your oats in milk overnight. **Serves 4**

2⅓ cups rolled oats
1¾ cups reduced-fat unsweetened coconut milk
3 tablespoons jaggery (palm sugar) or brown sugar
1 mango

Place the oats in a bowl, add the milk, and cover with plastic wrap. Leave in the refrigerator overnight.

Place the oat mixture and one and a half cups water in a pan. Add the sugar and slowly bring to a boil, stirring constantly. Reduce the heat, then simmer uncovered for about five minutes or until the mixture thickens.

Meanwhile, peel the mango and cut into thick slices, discarding the pit. Serve the coconut porridge topped with the sliced mango, or top with a little low-fat yogurt mixed with fresh vanilla.

Per serving: 342 Calories, 13g fat, 8g saturated fat, 0.1g sodium

Sofrito Spanish eggs

I've always loved the rustic cuisine of Spain: no fuss, no thrills, just good hearty food packed with plenty of flavor. Spanish smoked paprika is now widely available in stores, and is well worth making an effort to find, so look out for it. **Serves 4**

1 teaspoon olive oil
1 onion, finely chopped
1 garlic clove, crushed
2 ounces new potatoes, cooked, peeled and cut into ½-inch dice (about ⅓ cup)
2 ounces cooked lean ham, cut into ½-inch dice (about ½ cup)
½ teaspoon smoked paprika
One 14-ounce can tomatoes, finely chopped
½ cup fresh or frozen peas, cooked
1½ ounces chorizo sausage, thinly sliced (about ⅓ cup)
Freshly ground black pepper
4 small eggs
Oil-water spray (see page 33)

Preheat the oven to 325°F.

Heat the olive oil in a medium-sized non-stick pan. Add the onion, garlic, and two tablespoons water, cover with a lid, and sweat for two to three minutes until the onions are softened.

Add the potatoes and ham, then sprinkle the smoked paprika on top and cook for one minute to let the smoky paprika infuse the potatoes and ham.

Add the tomatoes, increase the heat, and cook until the tomatoes become thick and sauce-like in consistency, this should take about 10 minutes. Add the cooked peas and chorizo, and season with black pepper to taste.

Lightly spray four cocottes or custard cups with the oil-water spray, then divide the tomato mix between the cups. Using a small spoon, make an indentation in the center of each cup. Crack an egg carefully into the indentation. Season with black pepper.

Place the cups on a baking sheet and bake in the oven for 8–10 minutes or until the whites have set, but the yolks are still liquid.

Remove the dishes carefully on to individual serving plates, and serve with rustic country bread.

Per serving: 165 Calories, 9g fat, 3g saturated fat, 0.35g sodium

Soups and Salads

Thai gazpacho
A play on the classic Andalusian speciality of cold vegetable soup that traditionally contains garlic, tomatoes, and cucumbers. Here, I've included Asian flavors. The bread is used to provide bulk, although the consistency can be as light or as thick as you like. **Serves 4**

2 slices of white bread
14 ounces ripe but firm, tomatoes, coarsely chopped (about 2¼ cups)
1 onion, chopped
½ English cucumber
1 green pepper, seeded and chopped
2 garlic cloves, crushed
4 tablespoons red wine vinegar

2 lemongrass sticks, chopped
1 teaspoon red curry paste
1 kaffir lime leaf
10 Thai basil leaves, plus a few extra, for garnishing
⅔ cup tomato juice
1 teaspoon sugar
1-inch piece of fresh peeled root ginger, chopped
1 tablespoon ketchup

Soak the bread in water for 10 minutes, then squeeze out.

Place the bread in a large bowl, add the remaining ingredients, and stir well to combine. Let infuse in the refrigerator, preferably overnight.

Remove the lime leaf, then place the mixture in a blender and blitz to a fine purée. Strain through a coarse strainer, then return to the refrigerator until ready to serve.

Serve well chilled, topped with Thai basil leaves.

Per serving: 98 Calories, 1g fat, 0g saturated fat, 0.26g sodium

Persian minted onion soup
A soup with the typical Middle Eastern flavors of fragrant spices and fresh mint, this is great for all seasons — perfect as a light meal in the summer or a warming, aromatic appetizer in winter. Choose herbs that are as fresh as possible to maximize flavor. **Serves 4**

Oil-water spray (see page 33)
4 large onions, thinly sliced
1 teaspoon sugar
¼ teaspoon ground turmeric
⅛ teaspoon ground cinnamon
⅛ teaspoon ground cardamom
2 tablespoons flour

4 cups chicken stock (see page 39)
3 tablespoons lemon juice
3 tablespoons lime juice
2 tablespoons chopped mint leaves

Heat a squirt of oil-water spray in a heavy pot. Add the onions, sugar, turmeric, cinnamon, and cardamom, and four tablespoons water, cover with a lid, and cook over a medium heat for 10–15 minutes, stirring regularly until all the liquid has evaporated, leaving the onions tender, caramelized and golden in color.

Sprinkle the flour on top, and cook over a reduced heat for two minutes. Gradually add the chicken stock, stirring regularly, and then bring to a boil. Reduce the heat and simmer for 40 minutes.

Mix together the lemon and lime juice, then add to the soup and simmer for a further 10 minutes.

Stir in the mint, and serve immediately.

Per serving: 107 Calories, 1g fat, 0g saturated fat, 0.33g sodium

Smoked pumpkin and tortilla soup

A soup I actually created by accident, when, after a recent Halloween party for my youngest child, I came across an uncarved pumpkin. The smoked paprika gives it a warming flavor – just the trick for a winter's day! **Serves 4**

Oil-water spray (see page 33)
1¼ pounds pumpkin, skin and
    seeds removed, cut into
    small pieces
½ tablespoon smoked paprika
1 onion, chopped
1 leek, white part only,
    chopped
2 garlic cloves, crushed

4 corn tortillas, broken into
    small pieces
4 cups chicken or vegetable
    stock (see page 39)
½ cup skim milk
2 tablespoons chopped flat-
    leaf parsley
Freshly ground black pepper

Heat a squirt of oil-water spray in a non-stick pot. Dust the pumpkin pieces with the smoked paprika and fry in the pot, along with two tablespoons water, covered with a lid, to color them lightly, this should take about 10–12 minutes.

Add the onion, leek, garlic, and tortillas, replace the lid, and sweat the vegetables for a further 8–10 minutes.

Pour in the stock and bring to a boil, then reduce the heat to a simmer and cook for 20 minutes until the pumpkin is soft. Add the milk and stir well. Pour into a blender and blitz to a smooth purée, then return to the pot to reheat.

Add the parsley, season with black pepper to taste, and serve.

Per serving: 221 Calories, 5g fat, 1g saturated fat, 0.91g sodium

Chilled hummus, saffron, and yogurt soup

A wonderful chilled summer soup with flavors redolent of the eastern Mediterranean. Hummus means chickpea in Arabic, and is made by creating a paste with chickpeas and tahini. **Serves 4**

1 teaspoon olive oil
1 onion, chopped
2 garlic cloves, crushed
1 teaspoon ground cumin
Pinch of saffron
2 cups dried chickpeas, soaked overnight
3 cups vegetable stock (see page 39)
1 tablespoon tahini (sesame seed paste)
½ cup low-fat plain yogurt
Juice of 1 lemon
2 tablespoons chopped cilantro
Pinch of paprika
Freshly ground black pepper

Heat the oil in a pot, add the onion, garlic, cumin, and add two tablespoons water, then cover with a lid. Reduce the heat and cook for five minutes. Remove the lid, add the saffron, and cook for two more minutes. Add the drained chickpeas, cover with the vegetable stock, and return to the boil, then reduce the heat and cook for 40–45 minutes until the chickpeas are tender.

Pour into a blender, add the tahini, and blitz to a smooth paste.

Place in a bowl and chill thoroughly. Add the yogurt, lemon juice, and chopped cilantro. Season with black pepper to taste and serve chilled, sprinkled with paprika.

Per serving: 315 Calories, 8g fat, 2g saturated fat, 0.3g sodium

Chestnut and coconut milk soup with coriander

One of my favorite soups, with a hint of lemon and fresh cilantro. Chestnuts are usually found in stuffings, but the French use them often in soups. Vegetarians may replace the chicken stock with vegetable stock. **Serves 4**

2½ cups chicken stock (see page 39)
1 garlic clove, crushed
1 onion, chopped
1 leek, white part only, chopped
2 lemongrass sticks, finely chopped
⅓ cup long-grain rice
1 scant cup tinned unsweetened chestnut purée
1 cup reduced-fat unsweetened coconut milk
Juice of ½ lime
¼ cup roughly chopped cilantro
Freshly ground black pepper

Pour the chicken stock in a pot, along with the garlic, onion, leek, and lemongrass, and cook for 10 minutes. Add the rice, chestnut purée, and coconut milk, return to a boil, then reduce the heat and simmer for 20–25 minutes.

Remove from the heat, add the lime juice, then pour into a blender and blitz to a smooth purée. Add a little coconut milk if necessary, strain, and return to the pot to reheat.

Finally stir in the cilantro, season with black pepper to taste, and serve.

Per serving: 195 Calories, 8g fat, 6g saturated fat, 0.34g sodium

Hot-and-sour clam broth

An oriental-inspired light soup, both delicate and interesting in flavor. Here I use clams, a favorite ingredient of mine, but you could substitute mussels or mixed seafood if you prefer. Supermarkets now sell packages of cooked, mixed seafood for convenience. **Serves 4**

1 teaspoon sugar

1 tablespoon lime juice

1 tablespoon reduced-salt soy sauce

3 cups chicken stock (see page 39)

1 garlic clove, crushed

4 scallions, finely shredded

3 ounces shiitake mushrooms, sliced (about 1 cup)

1-inch piece of fresh peeled ginger root, thinly shredded

3 ounces pak choi, finely shredded (about 1½ cups)

1 lb. 2 oz. baby clams in their shells

½ teaspoon chili oil

Freshly ground black pepper

Mix together the sugar, lime juice, and soy sauce.

In a pot, bring the stock to a boil, add the vegetables and ginger, and simmer for 8–10 minutes. Add the clams and cook for a further two minutes, until they open. Add the sugar and juice mixture, and cook for a further minute.

Remove from the heat, add the chili oil, season to taste with black pepper, and serve in deep bowls.

Per serving: 49 Calories, 1g fat, 0g saturated fat, 0.48g sodium

Barley minestrone with pesto

An Italian-style vegetable soup that can make an impression all year round. You can vary the vegetables as you wish. The barley, which replaces the usual spaghetti or macaroni, adds a little chewiness to the soup. **Serves 4**

½ cup barley, soaked for 4 hours and drained

3 ounces green cabbage, roughly chopped (about 1½ cups)

1 onion, diced

1 carrot, diced

1 stalk celery, diced

1 zucchini, diced

4 tomatoes, deseeded, diced

1 baking potato, peeled, diced

½ cup frozen fava or, if unavailable, peas or baby limas

1 garlic clove, crushed

4 cups chicken stock (see page 39)

Freshly ground black pepper

For the pesto

Handful of fresh basil leaves

2 garlic cloves, crushed

Place the barley in a pan, cover with cold water, and bring to a boil. Cook for 25–30 minutes until tender, then drain.

In a large pot, combine all the vegetables with the stock and bring to a boil, then lower the heat and simmer for 15 minutes until the vegetables are just tender.

To make the pesto, place the basil and garlic in a blender, add a half-cup of the vegetable cooking liquid, and blitz to a smooth purée.

Add the purée to the soup, stir until combined, then add the cooked barley, season with black pepper, and serve.

Per serving: 164 Calories, 1g fat, 0g saturated fat, 0.35g sodium

Asopao (chicken paella soup)

This hearty soup, originating from Puerto Rico, is ideal for a one-pot meal. Traditionally, the soup contains a long list of ingredients, including rice, but everybody has their own combination, handed down over the years. Serve with lots of chunky bread. **Serves 4**

1 tablespoon unsaturated oil
1 large chicken breast, skinned, and cut into fine strips
1 small onion, finely chopped
2 garlic cloves, crushed
1 teaspoon chopped oregano (or pinch of dried)
¼ teaspoon dried chili flakes
1 cup canned chopped tomatoes
½ cup long-grain rice

1 red pepper, seeded and chopped
2 ounces cooked lean ham, chopped (½ cup)
3 cups chicken stock (see page 39)
1 tablespoon green olives, pitted and chopped
1 teaspoon superfine capers, rinsed and drained
½ cup cooked green peas
Freshly ground black pepper

Heat the oil in a non-stick pan, add the chicken strips, and fry over a high heat until golden. Lower the heat, add the onion, garlic, oregano, and chili flakes, and cook for two to three minutes.

Add the tomatoes, rice, red pepper, and ham.

Pour in the stock, bring to a boil, lower the heat, and simmer for 25–30 minutes.

Finally, add the olives, capers, and peas, adjust the seasoning with black pepper, and serve.

Per serving: 197 Calories, 5g fat, 1g saturated fat, 0.56g sodium

Shrimp tamarind soup

Using the classic bisque of France as a base, I added a little tamarind to give it a slight sharpness that really works well. If using frozen tiger shrimp, ensure that they are fully defrosted before use. A great soup for a dinner party. **Serves 4**

1 lb. 2 oz. fresh or frozen tiger shrimp, shelled and de-veined
1 onion, chopped
1 garlic clove, crushed
1 small red chile, seeded and chopped
1 tablespoon tomato paste
1 tablespoon all-purpose flour
4 tomatoes, chopped
1 tablespoon tamarind paste

2 lemongrass sticks, finely chopped
4 cups fish stock; see page 39 (or water)
1 tablespoon jaggery (palm sugar) or raw sugar
1 teaspoon nam pla (fish sauce)
Juice of ½ lime
Pinch of cayenne pepper
Oil-water spray (see page 33)

Heat a squirt of oil-water spray in a heavy pot. When hot, add the shrimp shells and fry until red, stirring them constantly. Remove and set aside.

Add the onion, garlic, and chile to the pan and fry for two to three minutes. Stir in the tomato paste and mix well.

Sprinkle in the flour, mix well, and cook for a further two minutes. Add the chopped tomatoes, tamarind paste, lemongrass, and stock, and bring to a boil, then reduce the heat and simmer for 30–35 minutes.

Strain through a fine mesh strainer into a clean pan and add the nam pla, lime juice, palm sugar, and cayenne.

Chop the shrimp roughly into bite-sized pieces and cook in the soup for one minute before serving.

Per serving: 173 Calories, 2g fat, 0g saturated fat, 0.67g sodium

Deviled caesar salad with crisp prosciutto and sundried tomatoes

Adding a little hot Tabasco or pepper sauce to the dressing gives a new twist to this classic salad that is both light and low in fat.
Serves 4

7 ounces new potatoes, peeled
 (about 4 medium)
4 slices prosciutto (Parma
 ham)
Oil-water spray (see page 33)
2 thick slices whole-grain bread
1 romaine lettuce, cut into
 pieces
2 anchovy fillets, canned,
 drained, rinsed, and finely
 chopped
3½ ounces sun-dried
 tomatoes in oil, drained
 (about ½ cup)
1 tablespoon grated Parmesan
 cheese

For the dressing
½ teaspoon Worcestershire
 sauce
1 teaspoon Dijon mustard
2 garlic cloves
1 tablespoon grated Parmesan
 cheese
½ cup low-fat plain yogurt
Dash of Tabasco or hot pepper
 sauce

Preheat the broiler to the highest setting.
Place the potatoes in a pan of boiling water and return to a boil, then cover, reduce the heat, and simmer for 10–12 minutes or until just tender.
Put the slices of prosciutto on a baking tray, and broil until crisp, then break into fairly large pieces.
Lightly spray the slices of bread with the oil-water spray and toast under the broiler until golden and crisp. Let cool, then cut into ½-inch cubes.
In a bowl, combine the lettuce, half the anchovies, the potatoes, tomatoes, and half the cheese, and mix gently. Top with the prosciutto and sprinkle the remaining cheese on top.
Mix the remaining anchovies with the dressing ingredients in a blender. Drizzle it over the salad and serve.

Per serving: 191 Calories, 5g fat, 2g saturated fat, 0.82g sodium

Chickpea, beet, and cauliflower salad, curried egg dressing
A simple and delicious salad containing lots of texture and flavor – the curry powder gives the vegetables an added zing. Easy to prepare; a real winner! **Serves 4**

12 baby beet with stems,
 washed
1 small cauliflower, separated
 into small florets
4 romaine lettuce leaves
3 ounces arugula leaves (about
 2 cups)
One 15-ounce can chickpeas,
 drained and rinsed
2 ounces freshly picked
 cilantro leaves (about
 1⅓ cups)

For the dressing
½ garlic clove, flattened with
 the back of a knife
1 teaspoon Dijon mustard
1 teaspoon mild curry powder
¼ cup reduced-calorie
 mayonnaise
Juice of ½ lemon
1 tablespoon half-fat crème
 fraîche (or, if unavailable,
 half-fat sour cream)
2 eggs, hard-boiled and
 chopped
Freshly ground black pepper

Preheat the oven to 400°F.
Place the beet in a pouch of foil with a half-cup water and scrunch up the foil to secure the beets within. Place in the oven for 40 minutes, or until tender when pierced with a small knife. Remove and let cool. When cool enough to handle, peel them.
Cook the cauliflower florets in boiling water until just tender, but firm, refresh in cold water, and drain well.
To make the dressing, rub the inside of a bowl with the garlic clove, and then discard it. Put the mustard, curry powder and mayonnaise in the bowl and mix well. Then add the lemon juice, a quarter-cup water, the crème fraîche and chopped egg, and season with black pepper to taste. The dressing should be thick, but still pourable.
Place all the leaves in a large bowl, add the beets, cauliflower, and chickpeas, and a little of the dressing. Serve on four plates, coating the cauliflower with a little more dressing, and scattering the cilantro on top.

Per serving: 252 Calories, 11g fat, 2g saturated fat, 0.44g sodium

Feta-baked flatbread and chickpea salad

Flatbread is available from good Italian delicatessens; it is sometimes called carta musica *or* music sheets, *as it is very thin. There are also many varieties of Middle Eastern-style flatbread which can be used.* **Serves 4**

4 sheets Sardinian flatbread, broken into large pieces

2 ounces feta cheese, crumbled (about ½ cup)

Freshly ground black pepper

One 15-ounce can chickpeas, drained and rinsed

7 ounces cherry tomatoes (about 1 heaped cup)

20 black olives, pitted

3 ounces flat-leaf parsley leaves (about 1½ cups

1 tablespoon pine nuts, toasted

2 bunches watercress

For the dressing

1 tablespoon tahini (sesame seed paste)

1 garlic clove, crushed

½ cup water

¼ cup low-fat plain yogurt

Juice of ½ lemon

Preheat the oven to 400°F.

Lay the flatbread on a large baking sheet, sprinkle the crumbled feta on top and bake for two to three minutes, until the cheese begins to melt.

In a bowl, whisk all the ingredients for the dressing together and season with black pepper to taste.

Place the chickpeas, tomatoes, olives, parsley, pine nuts, and watercress ingredients in another bowl, pour the dressing over them and toss lightly together.

Layer the salad with the flatbread, and serve.

Per serving: 257 Calories, 11g fat, 3g saturated fat, 0.83g sodium

Murgh chaat (spiced chicken and mango salad)

This is usually made with cooked chicken, but smoked chicken makes a nice alternative. Murgh means chicken and chaat, *means to savor, and this is indeed a tempting salad, ideal for the summer months.* **Serves 4**

Juice of 2 limes

Juice of ½ lemon

1 garlic clove, crushed

2 tablespoons maple syrup

1 cooked smoked chicken, skin removed, and meat shredded

2 ripe plum tomatoes, skinned, seeded, and chopped

1 green chile, seeded and very finely chopped

½ English cucumber, seeded and chopped

2 red onions, finely sliced

1 green pepper, seeded and chopped

1 teaspoon cumin seeds, lightly toasted

2 tablespoons roughly chopped cilantro

1 tablespoon roughly chopped mint

1 mango, peeled, and cut into wedges

Freshly ground black pepper

In a bowl, whisk the juice of the limes and lemon with the garlic and maple syrup. Add the remaining ingredients, and toss well together.

Marinate for 30 minutes before serving to let the flavors meld.

Per serving: 351 Calories, 16g fat, 5g saturated fat, 1.44g sodium

Wok-seared duck salad with lemongrass and ginger dressing

I love warm salads, especially ones that have an Oriental flavor. Chicken can be used instead of duck, if you prefer. Ketchap manis is the Indonesian soy sauce, made from black soybeans. **Serves 4**

1 teaspoon unsaturated oil

4 x 5-ounce duck breasts, skin removed

1 tablespoon brown sugar

¼ cup orange juice

2 tablespoons ketchap manis

1-inch piece of fresh ginger root, peeled

1 garlic clove

12 broccoli florets

5 ounces mixed salad greens (about 2½ cups)

1 carrot, finely shredded

3 ounces bean sprouts (about 1⅓ cups)

Freshly ground black pepper

¼ cup slivered almonds, toasted

For the dressing

2-inch piece of fresh ginger root

¼ cup orange juice

2 tablespoons balsamic vinegar

2 tablespoons ketchap manis

2 lemongrass sticks, finely chopped

1 garlic clove, crushed

1 tablespoon sweet chili sauce

To make the dressing, use a fine grater to grate the ginger into a bowl, then squeeze or strain through cheesecloth so you are left with the juice only. Add the remaining ingredients to the juice and season to taste. Set aside.

Heat the oil in a wok, add the duck breasts and seal all over. Then add the sugar, orange juice, ketchap manis, ginger, and garlic, and cook for 10–12 minutes, basting regularly until the duck is cooked and glazed all over. Remove and keep warm.

Cook the broccoli in boiling water.

Place the salad greens, broccoli, carrot, and bean sprouts in a bowl, add a little dressing, and toss well. Season with black pepper to taste.

Cut the duck into thin slices, top with salad, pour a little dressing over it and serve, scattered with the toasted almonds.

Per serving: 376 Calories, 18g fat, 3g saturated fat, 1.36g sodium

Spiced shrimp salad (pla talay)

A salad I have prepared for numerous dinner parties, with great success. Other shellfish, like lobster, could be substituted if you prefer. Nam pla (fish sauce) is available from major stores and Oriental supermarkets. **Serves 4**

2 tablespoons lime juice

1 tablespoon nam pla (fish sauce)

1 teaspoon sesame oil

2 tablespoons reduced-salt soy sauce

1 small red chile, seeded and finely chopped

½ garlic clove, crushed

1 teaspoon sugar

1 avocado

14 ounces fresh or frozen large tiger shrimp, cooked

2 lemongrass sticks, very finely shredded

2 shallots, thinly sliced

2 tablespoon finely shredded mint leaves

4 scallions, cut in half, and finely shredded lengthwise

1 green papaya, peeled and finely shredded (optional)

3½ ounces watercress (about 2 large handfuls)

In a bowl, mix together the lime juice, nam pla, sesame oil, and soy sauce, then add the chopped chile. Add the garlic and sugar, and mix well together.

Cut the avocado in half lengthwise, remove the pit, and cut in half again. Carefully peel off the outer skin and cut the flesh into long, thin slices. Add the shrimp and avocado to the bowl.

Add the remaining ingredients and carefully toss the lot together. Dress on individual plates and serve immediately.

Per serving: 215 Calories, 9g fat, 1g saturated fat, 2.21g sodium

Chilled noodle seafood salad

Most supermarkets sell cooked seafood, which, I have to say, is pretty good quality and certainly takes a lot of tedious preparation work out of the dish. This is a simple but satisfying salad, perfect for the summer months. **Serves 4**

9 ounces tagliatelle

9-ounce package cooked
   seafood selection

4 scallions, shredded

2 plum tomatoes, seeded and
   chopped

¼ English cucumber, chopped

Freshly ground black pepper

2 tablespoons roughly
   chopped dill

For the dressing

½ teaspoon Dijon mustard

½ garlic clove, crushed

Juice of 1 lemon

1 tablespoon olive oil

1 teaspoon honey

First make the dressing by placing the mustard and garlic in a large bowl. Add the lemon juice, olive oil, and honey, whisking well to amalgamate.

Cook the pasta in boiling water until tender and *al dente*, drain well, then add to the dressing and toss thoroughly together. (Adding the pasta when hot allows it to absorb the flavors in the dressing.) Add the seafood, scallions, tomatoes, and cucumber, season with black pepper to taste, and let cool to room temperature.

Add the dill and toss before serving.

Per serving: 320 Calories, 5g fat, 1g saturated fat, 0.5 sodium

Smoked trout, orange, and blueberry salad with arugula and tarragon

The combination of smoked fish and fruit is legendary since the fruit not only counteracts the richness of the fish, but also gives a pleasant freshness to the salad. **Serves 4**

6 sweet navel oranges

2 tablespoons sugar

2 teaspoons Dijon mustard

2 teaspoons arrowroot,
   dissolved in ¼ cup cold
   water

2 tablespoons chopped fresh
   tarragon

9 ounces blueberries (about
   1½ cups)

2 tablespoons pine nuts,
   toasted

11 ounces arugula leaves
   (about 2½-3 cups)

14 ounces smoked trout, skin
   removed and flaked

Squeeze the juice from two of the oranges. Place in a non-stick pan, add the sugar and mustard, and bring to a boil. Whisk in the dissolved arrowroot, reduce the heat, and stir until thickened. Let cool.

Using a small knife, peel the remaining oranges, ensuring all the white pith is removed. Quarter the oranges lengthwise, then cut crosswise into thick slices.

Place in a bowl, add the orange and arrowroot mixture, tarragon, blueberries, pine nuts, and arugula, and toss to coat. Sprinkle the flaked smoked trout over it, and serve.

Per serving: 286 Calories, 9g fat, 1g saturated fat, 0.79g sodium

Light Meals and Appetizers

3

Artichokes provençale

Artichokes are a fiddly vegetable to prepare, I will admit, since you have to get past their tough bracts and chokes, but once you've mastered their preparation, you'll love to try cooking them in lots of different ways. This dish is also great served cold. **Serves 4**

4 artichokes

2 teaspoons olive oil

¼ cup dry white wine

1 garlic clove, crushed

14 ounces ripe plum tomatoes, skinned, seeded and cut into ½-inch dice (about 1½ cups)

2 sprigs of thyme

Freshly ground black pepper

Pinch of sugar

16 black olives

2 tablespoons pine nuts

12 fresh basil leaves, chopped

Cut the artichoke stalk an inch below the artichoke's base. Remove the fibrous, dark green outer leaves until the tender, yellowish-green inner leaves are revealed. Cut off between one- and two-thirds from the top of the artichoke, leaving about an inch of leaves above the base. Using a small knife, trim the base, and cut off the remaining tough, dark green leaves to expose the tightly packed central leaves that conceal the hairy center choke. Scoop out the raw choke with a teaspoon.

Place the artichokes upside down in a non-stick pan. Whisk together the olive oil, wine, and two-thirds cup water, and pour over the artichokes. Bring to a boil and add the garlic, chopped tomatoes, thyme, black pepper, and sugar.

Reduce the heat to low, cover with a lid, and cook until the artichokes are all tender, this should take about 20 minutes. Remove the lid, discard the thyme, add the olives, pine nuts, and basil, adjust the seasoning, and serve.

Per serving: 184 Calories, 8g fat, 1g saturated fat, 0.46g sodium

Grilled asparagus and leeks mimosa

Despite the implications of its name, buttermilk is much lower in fat than ordinary milk, commercially made by a similar method to that used for yogurt. It has a slightly sour taste that makes it more interesting than plain skim milk. **Serves 4**

14 ounces asparagus, trimmed (about 14-18 spears)

7 ounces baby leeks

Freshly ground black pepper

2 teaspoons olive oil

For the mimosa dressing

1 tablespoon white wine vinegar

1 teaspoon Dijon mustard

2 tablespoons chopped fresh tarragon

3 tablespoons buttermilk

1 teaspoon sugar

2 eggs, hard-boiled and chopped

2 tablespoons olive oil

To make the dressing, whisk together the vinegar and mustard in a bowl. Add the tarragon, buttermilk, sugar, and eggs, and blend in the oil.

In separate pans, blanch the asparagus and leeks in boiling water for two minutes, then remove and drain. Place in a shallow dish and season with black pepper. Pour the olive oil over them, toss, and let cool.

Heat a ridged grill pan until very hot, add the leeks and asparagus, and cook for four to five minutes until charred, turning them regularly to ensure an even coloring.

Remove to a serving dish, pour the mimosa dressing on top, and serve warm.

Per serving: 142 Calories, 11g fat, 2g saturated fat, 0.08g sodium

Stuffed eggplant with tomato and bulgur pilaf

This always makes an impressive-looking dish, stuffed with all sorts of ingredients. Bulgur or cracked wheat is a staple of the Balkan countries where it is used as a cheaper alternative to rice. **Serves** 4

4 medium eggplants
2 garlic cloves, thinly sliced
½ teaspoon olive oil
1 red onion, chopped
1 tablespoon thyme leaves
5 ounces sun-blush tomatoes
¼ cup raisins
5 ounces dried bulgur (cracked wheat), cooked

2 tablespoons pine nuts, toasted
1 tablespoon roughly chopped cilantro
2 ounces half-fat Cheddar cheese, grated (about ½ cup)
Freshly ground black pepper

Preheat the oven to 400°F.

With a sharp knife, make slits all over the eggplants and, using half the garlic, stud a slice of garlic into each slit. Wrap the eggplants in a large sheet of foil and seal the foil. Place on a baking sheet and cook in the oven for 30 minutes. When cooked, remove from the foil, cut in half horizontally, and let cool completely.

Remove the eggplant flesh from the centers, leaving enough outer wall to keep the eggplants intact. Chop the flesh into large dice.

Heat the olive oil in a non-stick pan, add the onion, remaining garlic, and the thyme. Cook until lightly golden.

Add the eggplant flesh, tomatoes, raisins, the cooked bulgur and a half-cup water, cover with a lid, and cook over low heat for 10 minutes. Add the pine nuts, the cilantro, and Cheddar. Season with black pepper to taste.

Fill the eggplant casings with the mix, place on a baking sheet, return to the oven, and bake for 15 minutes.

Per serving: 301 Calories, 8g fat, 2g saturated fat, 0.41g sodium

Chickpea dolmades

Traditionally these vine-leaf wraps are filled with ground meat, but vegetarians will be happy with this chickpea substitute. If using brine-soaked vine leaves, blanch in boiling water for one minute to remove their saltiness. The wraps can be made up to a day ahead, if you wish. **Serves** 4

20 fresh vine leaves
1 tablespoon olive oil
1 onion, finely chopped
1 garlic clove, crushed
2 ounces mint, chopped (1⅓ cups)
3½ ounces feta cheese, crumbled (a scant cup)
One 15-ounce can chickpeas, drained and rinsed
¼ cup pine nuts
¾ cup brown rice, cooked
½ teaspoon ground cumin
¼ cup currants
Oil-water spray (see page 33)

For the tomato tartare
11 ounces ripe plum tomatoes, seeded and cut into ½-inch dice (a heaped cup)
1 tablespoon maple syrup
Juice of ½ small lemon
2 tablespoons chopped cilantro
2 tablespoons chopped flat-leaf parsley
1 garlic clove, crushed

For the yogurt sauce
½ cup low-fat plain yogurt
2 tablespoons chopped mint
½ teaspoon grated lemon peel
1 tablespoon honey

Preheat the oven to 350°F.

Blanch the vine leaves for three to four minutes in boiling water until tender. Drain well and pat dry on paper towels.

Heat the olive oil in a pan, add the onion, garlic, and two tablespoons water, cover, and cook over low heat for 3-4 minutes. Uncover, add the mint, half the feta, chickpeas, pine nuts, rice, cumin, currants, and cook for 2-3 minutes. Let cool slightly.

Place the vine leaves, shiny side down, on the counter. Spoon some of the rice filling in the center and fold the stalk end over the filling. Roll up the wrap towards the tip of the leaf, tucking in the sides. Lightly grease a baking tray with the oil-water spray, sprinkle the remaining feta cheese over it, and place under a preheated broiler to melt for one to two minutes.

To make the tartare, mix together all the ingredients in a bowl, and in a separate bowl, do the same for the yogurt sauce.

Dress the grilled vine leaves with the tomato tartare, drizzle a little yogurt sauce on top, and serve.

Per serving: 410 Calories, 20g fat, 5g saturated fat, 0.54g sodium

"Wild" baguette with mozzarella cheese fondue

A tastier version of cheese on toast, this makes a great snack at any time of the day. If you find wild mushrooms a little expensive or hard to come by, replace with another variety; the dish will be equally delicious. **Serves 4**

½ large French baguette
1 teaspoon olive oil
7 ounces selection of wild mushrooms, thickly sliced (about 2 cups)
2 shallots, finely chopped
½ garlic clove, roasted
2 ounces arugula, chopped (about 1⅓ cups)
2 tablespoons roughly chopped flat-leaf parsley
Freshly ground black pepper

For the mozzarella fondue

⅔ cup low fat milk
1 garlic clove, crushed
2 tablespoons cornstarch
Pinch of paprika
½ teaspoon Dijon mustard
3 ounces half-fat mozzarella cheese, grated (about ¾ cup)

Preheat the broiler to its highest setting.

Cut the baguette in half, then in half horizontally to create bread bases.

Heat the olive oil in a non-stick frying pan, then add the mushrooms, shallots, and garlic, and cook for three to four minutes, until tender and golden. Add the chopped arugula and parsley, season with black pepper, and keep warm.

To make the fondue, boil the milk with the garlic in a pan. Dilute the cornstarch with two tablespoons water, and whisk into the milk. Cook for two minutes, then add the paprika and mustard. Remove from the heat and stir in the grated mozzarella. Stir until the cheese has melted into the sauce.

Toast the baguettes under the broiler, top with the mushrooms, drizzle the cheese fondue over them, and serve.

Per serving: 235 Calories, 5g fat, 2g saturated fat, 0.35g sodium

Grilled portobello burger with ricotta and arugula slaw

A great vegetarian burger using juicy Portobello mushrooms that have an almost meaty flavor of their own. Good for summer barbecues where vegetarians needn't feel left out. **Serves 4**

4 medium/large Portobello mushrooms, stalks removed
2 garlic cloves, peeled
1 teaspoon thyme leaves
2 tablespoons balsamic vinegar
1 teaspoon olive oil
4 traditional burger buns, split open

For the herbed ricotta

1 tablespoon pesto
¼ cup ricotta cheese

For the rocket slaw

3 ounces arugula (about 2 cups)
1 tablespoon balsamic vinegar
2 tablespoons reduced-calorie mayonnaise
2 scallions, shredded
1 small carrot, peeled and sliced
1 tablespoon honey

Clean and peel the mushrooms. Using a small paring knife, cut slits into the mushrooms.

Cut the garlic cloves into thin slices, then push into the holes in the mushrooms. Place in a dish, sprinkle the thyme over them, pour the vinegar and oil over them, and let marinate for one hour.

Meanwhile, to make the herbed ricotta, mix the pesto with the ricotta and set aside. Mix all the ingredients for the arugula slaw together in a bowl.

Heat a ridged grill pan and when smoking, add the mushrooms and grill for three to four minutes on each side until soft, cooked, and slightly charred all over. Remove, then toast the buns until lightly charred, this should take two to three minutes.

Spread the buns with the herbed ricotta and add a grilled Portobello. Top with a spoonful of arugula slaw, then replace the bun lid and serve. Oven fries (see page 101) are a classic accompaniment.

Per serving: 236 Calories, 9g fat, 3g saturated fat, 0.39g sodium

Shiitaki mushroom noodles with Asian pesto

Pesto is a classic Italian sauce redolent of garlic, lots of basil, and Parmesan. My Asian variety uses mint and cilantro spiced with ginger and is great for a salad dressing or served with grilled fish. **Serves 4**

14 ounces Chinese egg noodles
1 tablespoon sesame oil
4½ ounces shiitake mushrooms, thickly sliced (about 1½ cups)
1 garlic clove, crushed
½-inch piece of fresh ginger root, peeled and finely chopped
1 green chile, seeded and thinly sliced
4 scallions, shredded
3 tablespoons reduced-salt soy sauce

For the pesto

1½ ounces (about 1 cup) mint leaves
1½ ounces cilantro (about 1 cup)
1 garlic clove, crushed
3 tablespoons roasted peanuts
1-inch piece ginger root, peeled and finely chopped
1 tablespoon olive oil
Pinch of sugar

To make the pesto, place all the ingredients in a blender, blitz to a coarse purée, and set aside.

Soak the noodles for three to four minutes in a bowl of boiling water, then drain them well.

In a large non-stick pan or wok, heat the sesame oil until very hot, then add the sliced shiitake mushrooms and sauté for one minute or until they are slightly softened. Add the garlic, ginger, and chile, and continue to stir-fry. Add the scallions and soy sauce and toss together.

Add the drained noodles and the pesto, toss together until heated through, and serve.

Per serving: 499 Calories, 17g fat, 3g saturated fat, 0.66g sodium

Menemen (Turkish scrambled eggs)

This recipe comes courtesy of a friend who took a lot of persuading to divulge it. It's a great way to start the day or an ideal snack for lunchtime, served with traditional Turkish bread. Adding a little diced feta is good but will raise the fat count. **Serves 4**

1 teaspoon olive oil
1 onion, finely chopped
½ garlic clove, crushed
1 teaspoon harissa (hot spice paste)
1 small eggplant, cut into ½-inch cubes
1 small green pepper, seeded and cut into ½-inch cubes
2 plum tomatoes, cut into ½-inch cubes
2 large fresh eggs from free-range hens
Freshly ground black pepper
Good pinch of saffron, dissolved in 2 tablespoons boiling water
2 tablespoons chopped cilantro

Heat the olive oil in a medium-sized non-stick frying pan. Add the onion, garlic, and harissa, and cook over low heat for one to two minutes until softened, stirring regularly. Add the vegetables and cook for 10–15 minutes.

Meanwhile, in a bowl whisk the eggs with black pepper and add the saffron water.

When the vegetables are cooked, increase the heat, add the eggs, and let them set slightly before stirring them, to make chunky scrambled eggs around the vegetables. Add the cilantro and more pepper to taste. Serve with Middle-Eastern-style bread.

Per serving: 89 Calories, 5g fat, 1g saturated fat, 0.06g sodium

Indo-chine stir-fried rice with paneer and cashews

Everyone loves rice and has their preferred cooking method, but I especially love the Oriental way of stir-frying it. Paneer is a curd cheese, which can be substuted with ricotta or pot cheese, if necessary.. **Serves 4**

1 tablespoon unsaturated oil
3 cardamom pods, cracked
½ teaspoon ground cinnamon
2 scallions, chopped
1 red chile, seeded and finely
   chopped
⅓ cup ready-to-eat dried
   apricots, chopped
3 tablespoons golden raisins

1 teaspoon curry powder
1¾ cups basmati rice, cooked
2 ounces paneer (curd cheese),
   cut into ½-inch dice (about
   ½ cup)
½ cup fresh cashew nuts,
   chopped and toasted
1 ounce mint, chopped (about
   ⅔ cup)

Heat a large non-stick frying pan or wok and add the oil, spices, scallions and chile, and cook for one minute. Add the apricots, raisins and curry powder, and cook for one minute. **Add** the cooked rice, paneer, and cashews, and toss together for two to three minutes. Remove to a serving bowl and sprinkle with the mint before serving.

Per serving: 273 Calories, 11g fat, 2g saturated fat, 0.07g sodium

Pa-ad tofu

This vegetarian stir-fried rice noodle dish is one of countless Thai variations on a theme, both interesting and tasty, and the tofu provides valuable soy protein. Pickled white radish is available in cans and can be found in Asian grocery stores. **Serves 4**

11 ounces vermicelli rice
   noodles
1 tablespoon peanut oil
2 garlic cloves, crushed
½ tablespoon finely chopped
   fresh ginger root
1 red chile, thinly sliced
11 ounces Chinese broccoli,
   trimmed and chopped into
   pieces (about 3½-4 cups)
1¾ cups bean sprouts
2 tablespoons chopped pickled
   white radish

1 tablespoon brown sugar
2 tablespoons reduced-salt
   soy sauce
1 tablespoon sweet chili sauce
4 scallions, shredded
6 ounces firm tofu (half a
   12-ounce cake)
2 tablespoons roughly
   chopped cilantro
2 tablespoons chopped roasted
   peanuts
Freshly ground black pepper

Place the rice noodles in a bowl, cover with boiling water, let soften, and then drain them well.
In a wok or large non-stick frying pan, heat the peanut oil, add the garlic, ginger, and chile, and stir-fry for one minute.
Add the broccoli, bean sprouts, and radish, and cook for a further minute. Add the sugar, soy and chili sauces, and toss well together.
Throw in the scallions, tofu, cilantro, and peanuts. Season with black pepper to taste and serve in bowls.

Per serving: 401 Calories, 8g fat, 1g saturated fat, 0.34g sodium

Wasabi tuna tartare with cucumber and orange, and beet syrup

I love the freshness and contrasts of flavor in this dish, first the sweet beet syrup, then the hot wasabi horseradish that adds a punch to the raw tuna tartare. **Serves 4**

For the tartare
6 ounces very fresh tuna fillet, cut into ¼-inch dice (about ¾ cup)
1 shallot, finely chopped
Peel and juice of 1 orange
3 ounces cucumber, peeled and seeded, cut into ¼-inch dice (about ¾ cup)
2 tablespoons chopped cilantro, plus extra for garnishing
½ teaspoon wasabi paste
1 tablespoon chopped chives
2 tablespoons reduced-salt soy sauce
Freshly ground black pepper

For the beet syrup
2 raw beets
5 tablespoons sherry vinegar or red wine vinegar
½ teaspoon Dijon mustard

To make the beet syrup, peel the beets (I suggest you wear a pair of rubber gloves if you have them!), place in a juicer, and extract the juice. Place the juice in a pan, along with the vinegar and bring to a boil, skimming off any impurities that rise to the surface. Boil until the liquid has reduced by half. Pour into a bowl and let cool. Whisk in the mustard and season with black pepper to taste, then set aside.

To make the tartare, place the tuna in a bowl, add the remaining ingredients, and season with black pepper to taste. Place a two and a half inch cookie cutter on a serving plate, fill with the mix, press down well, then carefully remove the ring. Prepare the remaining three in the same way.

Pour some beet syrup around each tartare, garnish with the cilantro, and serve chilled.

Per serving: 85 Calories, 2g fat, 1g saturated fat, 0.39g sodium

Dhal cakes on Asian-style panzanella

Don't be put off by the large list of ingredients in this recipe; it is simple to prepare and a vegetarian delight. The cakes may be prepared in advance and cooked when needed. A wonderful dish for the summer months. **Serves 4**

¾ cup split yellow lentils, soaked overnight

1 teaspoon olive oil

1 garlic clove, crushed

1 green chile, seeded and finely chopped

½ teaspoon ground cumin

1-inch piece of fresh ginger root, finely chopped

¾ cup couscous

3 ounces spinach, chopped and cooked (about ¾ cup)

⅓ cup low-fat cottage cheese

2 scallions, chopped

2 tablespoons chopped mint

Oil-water spray (see page 33)

For the asian panzanella

1 tablespoon honey

1 mango, peeled and cut into ½-inch dice

1 nan bread, cut into ½-inch pieces

Juice of 2 limes

1 red pepper, seeded, and cut into ½-inch dice

½ garlic clove, crushed

1 green chile, seeded and finely chopped

2 tablespoons chopped cilantro

For the mint dressing

1 tablespoon mint jelly, melted

½ cup soy yogurt

Drain the soaked lentils. Heat the oil in a non-stick pan, add the garlic, chile, and cumin, and cook for one minute to release their fragrance. Add the lentils, ginger, and a quarter-cup water, then cover and cook for 10–15 minutes or until the lentils are tender and all the liquid has been absorbed.

Meanwhile, boil one and a half cups water and pour it over the couscous, cover with plastic wrap and let stand for four to five minutes. Fluff the couscous with a fork and let it swell for five more minutes, until all the liquid is completely absorbed. Remove the plastic wrap and let it cool completely.

Place the lentils and the couscous in a blender, add the chopped spinach, mix well, then, in short bursts, pulse to a coarse pulp. Do not purée completely. Remove the mix to a bowl, add the cottage cheese, scallions, and mint, mix well, and place in the fridge.

Preheat the broiler to the highest setting.

Divide the mix into patties. Lightly spray a baking tray with the oil-water spray, then arrange the patties on the tray.

Broil the patties for two to three minutes on each side.

Meanwhile, to make the panzanella, mix all the ingredients together in a bowl.

To make the dressing, mix together the mint jelly and yogurt.

To serve, arrange the panzanella on a large serving dish, top with the grilled dhal cakes, and drizzle with the mint dressing.

Per serving: 461 Calories, 9g fat, 3g saturated fat, 0.25g sodium

Steamed mussels with fragrant Asian spices

Mussels are a delicate mollusk; they need a minimum of cooking to retain their juicy and moist flavors. The addition of some basic Indian spices leaves the kitchen filled with heady aromas. **Serves 4**

1 teaspoon cumin seeds

2 teaspoons cardamom pods, cracked

2¼ pounds very fresh mussels, cleaned, and beards removed

2 shallots, finely chopped

½ cup dry white wine

1-inch piece of fresh ginger root, peeled and finely chopped

1 green chile, seeded and finely chopped

2 tablespoons roughly chopped cilantro

Heat a large non-stick wok (with a tight-fitting lid). Add the cumin seeds and cardamom pods, and cook for 30 seconds to release their fragrance.

Throw in the mussels, add the shallots, white wine, ginger, and chile and two-thirds cup water. Cover with the lid, bring to a boil rapidly and steam the mussels for two to three minutes until they open.

Add the cilantro and toss well together. Discard any unopened mussels and serve in a deep bowl with the broth poured over them.

Per serving: 84 Calories, 2g fat, 0g saturated fat, 0.22g sodium

Mackerel tartare in tomato shells

This is a light meal in itself, but can be a great appetizer for a dinner party since it can be prepared up to two hours ahead of time, leaving you plenty of time for your guests. Tuna or salmon could easily be used instead. **Serves 4**

8 medium/large salad tomatoes

Freshly ground black pepper

¼ cup olive oil

2 x 12-ounce very fresh mackerel, cleaned and filleted

1 teaspoon Dijon mustard

Juice of 2 lemons

1 small head fennel, very finely chopped

2 shallots, finely chopped

2 tablespoons chopped fresh mint

2 tablespoons chopped fresh tarragon leaves

2 tablespoons chopped fresh chives

1 small cooked beet, peeled and very finely chopped

Preheat the oven to 350°F.

Carefully slice the tops off of the tomatoes and scoop out the flesh and seeds and discard. Dry the insides of the tomatoes gently with paper towels, and season with black pepper. Brush inside and out with one tablespoon of the olive oil, and cook in the oven for five to eight minutes until they are just softened, but still retaining their shape. Remove and let cool.

Cut the mackerel fillet into ½-inch dice and place in a bowl. Add the mustard, lemon juice, fennel, remaining olive oil, the shallots, and herbs, and gently toss together. Add the beet and season with pepper to taste.

Fill the tomato shells with the mackerel tartare. Serve with a fresh green salad.

Per serving: 462 Calories, 35g fat, 6g saturated fat, 0.16g sodium

Ceviche of salmon and shellfish

Ceviche is a Central and South American specialty, in which raw fish is marinated in lime or lemon juice, and is a healthy way to start a dinner party. If you can't find fresh wild salmon, use farmed salmon, although the flavor will not be as good. **Serves 4**

2 beefsteak tomatoes
2 fresh red chiles, seeded and chopped
Juice of 2 limes
1 teaspoon coriander seeds, crushed
½ cup tomato juice
½ teaspoon sugar
Tabasco sauce
Freshly ground black pepper
11 ounces fresh wild salmon fillet, skinned
9 ounces cooked seafood selection
2 ounces cucumber, peeled, seeded, and diced (about ½ cup)
4 scallions, chopped
1 tablespoon chopped cilantro
Sprigs of cilantro and lime wedges, for garnishing

Preheat the broiler to its highest setting.

Cut one of the tomatoes in half, place the cut side down on a baking tray, and broil until the skins blacken. Turn over and blacken the other side. Remove and let cool.

Soak the remaining tomato in boiling water for about one minute, then remove with a slotted spoon. Peel away the skin, seed it, and dice it. Set aside.

Blend the charred tomato with the chiles, lime juice, coriander seeds, tomato juice, sugar, and a dash of Tabasco, until puréed and smooth, then season with pepper. Strain through a fine mesh strainer into a bowl.

Cut the salmon into thin slices and season lightly with pepper. Place in the bowl with the marinade, add the shellfish, cover with plastic wrap and marinate in the refrigerator for two hours.

Remove the salmon and shellfish from the marinade and arrange on four plates. Add the cucumber, scallions, chopped cilantro, and reserved diced tomato to the marinade and pour a little over the fish.

Garnish each plate with a cilantro leaf and a wedge of lime, and serve chilled.

Per serving: 229 Calories, 9g fat, 2g saturated fat, 0.75g sodium

Thin sardine tart
A delicate and light tart base, topped with sardines – a play on the classic pissaladière *from southern France. Phyllo is less fattening than puff pastry dough, and it is wonderfully crispy. Altogether a great appetizer or lunchtime dish, redolent with the flavors of Provence.* **Serves 4**

Oil-water spray (see page 33)
4 phyllo pastry dough sheets
1 tablespoon olive oil
1 large onion, thinly sliced
2 garlic cloves, crushed
1 tablespoon black olives, pitted and roughly chopped
2 canned anchovy fillets, drained, rinsed, and finely chopped
8 fresh sardines, cleaned, scaled, and filleted
1 teaspoon fresh thyme leaves
2 tablespoons chopped fresh parsley

Preheat the oven to 400°F.

Warm a 9-inch baking pan or pizza pan in the oven. Remove and spray with the oil-water spray.

Place one sheet of phyllo in the pan, then lightly spray all over, top with a second sheet, spray again, top with a third sheet, spray again, then top with the last sheet. Place in the oven for two to three minutes, then remove. Crumple up the excess pastry overhanging the pan to form a rim.

Heat the olive oil in a large non-stick pan, add the onion, garlic, and olives, and cook over medium heat for 10–12 minutes until the onions are soft, golden, and caramelized. Remove from the pan, add the anchovies, and mix well.

Wipe out the pan. Return to the heat and squirt with a little oil-water spray. Fry the sardine fillets for two to three minutes until golden and lightly crisp.

Spread the onion mix evenly over the phyllo base, then arrange the cooked sardine fillets on top. Scatter the thyme over them and return to the oven for two to three minutes.

Sprinkle the parsley on top and serve on a large dish, along with a bowl of green salad.

Per serving: 310 Calories , 14g fat, 3g saturated fat, 0.44g sodium

Main Courses

4

Spicy eggplant and shiitake stew

A simply prepared dish, packed with flavor. Stews are a good way to cook vegetables since their nutrients are retained in the liquid. The shiitake mushroom may be replaced with any mushroom variety, but shiitakes will instill a meaty flavor to this dish. **Serves 4**

1 tablespoon sesame oil

2 garlic cloves, crushed

1-inch piece of fresh ginger root, peeled and finely chopped

7 ounces shiitake mushrooms, thickly sliced (about 2 cups)

3 tablespoons dry sherry

2 tablespoons ketchap manis (Indonesian soy sauce)

2 tablespoons black bean sauce

2 large eggplants, cut into 1-inch dice

One 14½-ounce can water chestnuts, sliced

2½ cups vegetable stock (see page 39)

½ cup tomato juice

Heat a wok or large frying pan, add the sesame oil, garlic, ginger, and mushrooms, and cook over high heat for one to two minutes.

Add the sherry, ketchap manis, and black bean sauce, and mix well together. Add the eggplants and water chestnuts, and mix well again. Cook for three to four minutes, then add the stock and tomato juice. Cover with a lid, reduce the heat, and simmer for five to eight minutes until the vegetables are cooked, but still retain their shape, and the sauce is reduced in consistency.

Serve with a bowl of steaming white rice.

Per serving: 97 Calories, 4g fat, 0g saturated fat, 0.83g sodium

Indian vegetable crumble Serves 4

1 small cauliflower, separated into florets

1 onion, chopped

2 garlic cloves, crushed

2-inch piece of ginger root

1 hot green chile, seeded and finely chopped

Oil-water spray (see page 33)

2 tablespoons tandoori spice mix

3½ ounces paneer (curd cheese), drained and diced (about 1 cup)

2 carrots, cut into batons

1 red pepper, seeded, diced

1 green pepper, seeded, diced

1 baking potato, peeled, diced

One 15-ounce can chickpeas, drained and rinsed

2 tablespoons roughly chopped cilantro

For the crumble crust

A scant cup fresh cashew nuts

½ teaspoon mild curry powder

2 ounces cooked millet seed (about ⅓ cup)

1 teaspoon olive oil

For the mint yogurt sauce

½ cup low-fat plain yogurt

2 tablespoons roughly chopped mint

1 tablespoon lemon juice

Pinch of ground cumin

Preheat oven to 375°F.

Cook the cauliflower florets for five minutes in a pan of boiling water. Remove and refresh in cold water, drain, and dry well. Place the onion, garlic, ginger, and green chile in a blender with a quarter-cup water and blitz to a purée.

In a non-stick pan, heat a squirt of oil-water spray, then add the tandoori spice and paneer, and cook for one minute.

Add the cauliflower and remaining vegetables, the chickpeas, and mix well together. Add a quarter-cup water, cover, and simmer for six to eight minutes. Add the garlic and chile mixture, and cook uncovered until the vegetables are all coated in spices, this should take about five minutes. Transfer the vegetables to a small gratin or baking dish, suitable for oven-to-table use.

To make the crumble crust, coarsely blitz the cashews with the curry powder, millet, and olive oil, in a blender.

Sprinkle the mix evenly over the vegetables, then bake in the oven for 12–15 minutes, until the crust is golden and crispy.

Mix the sauce ingredients together. Remove the crumble from the oven, scatter with the chopped cilantro, and serve with the yogurt mint sauce.

Per serving: 463 Calories, 21g fat, 4g saturated fat, 0.34g sodium

Baked corn and vegetable tacos

These rolled tacos filled with vegetables are ideal for preparing ahead. Simply make them up the night before, then pop them in the oven when needed. Flour tortillas may be used instead of making corn crêpes, if time is of the essence. **Serves 4**

1 pound mixed vegetables
(e.g., parsnips, carrots,
butternut squash, zucchini)
2 tablespoons honey
1 tablespoon olive oil
1 red chile, seeded and finely
chopped
Freshly ground black pepper
Oil-water spray (see page 33)

2 cups passata sauce or
tomato sauce
2 ounces half-fat Cheddar
cheese, grated (about ½ cup)
For the pancakes
1 large egg
½ cup soy milk
1 tablespoon olive oil
⅓ cup finely ground cornmeal
6 tablespoons all-purpose flour

Preheat the oven to 400°F.

Peel the vegetables and cut into large wedges. Tip into a baking pan. Warm the honey, olive oil, and chile together and pour over the vegetables. Toss well, then season with pepper.

Place in the oven and roast for 40–45 minutes, until golden and slightly caramelized.

To make the crêpes, lightly beat the egg with the milk, olive oil, and a quarter-cup water. Sift in the cornmeal and flour, then gradually mix with the liquid to form a smooth batter. Strain and set aside.

Heat a small non-stick crêpe or omelette pan. Squirt with a little oil-water spray, then pour two tablespoons of batter into the center of the pan, tilting it quickly so that it spreads into a circle. Cook for one minute on each side, loosening the edges of the crêpe with a spatula. Slip on to a plate. Prepare seven more crêpes in the same way.

Divide the roasted vegetables between the eight crêpes and roll them up tightly. Arrange the crêpes, seam-side down, in a baking dish. Pour the passata sauce over them, then sprinkle the cheese on top. Bake in the oven until heated through, and the cheese has melted and is bubbling. Serve.

Per serving: 281 Calories, 12g fat, 3g saturated fat, 0.35g sodium

Three-squash ratatouille

I have always been a lover of squash and there are so many varieties available throughout the year. Butternut and turban squash are both winter varieties, which are good sources of iron and vitamins A and C. This makes a great vegetarian meal, served with rice. **Serves 4**

2 teaspoons olive oil
3 scallions, chopped
3 garlic cloves
1 green pepper, seeded and cut
into 1-inch dice
9 ounces butternut squash,
seeded and cut into 1-inch
dice (about 2 cups)
9 ounces turban squash,
seeded and cut into 1-inch
dice (about 2 cups)

2 zucchini, thickly sliced
One 14½-ounce can
tomatoes, chopped
1 tablespoon tomato paste
1 tablespoon sugar
1 bay leaf
1 tablespoon chopped basil
1 teaspoon thyme leaves
Peel of ½ lemon
Freshly ground black pepper

Preheat the oven to 325°F.

Heat the olive oil in an ovenproof non-stick pan, add the scallions, garlic, and green pepper, and cook over medium heat for three to four minutes or until tender.

Add all the squash and zucchini, cover with a lid, and cook for a further five minutes. Add the tomatoes and their juice and the rest of the ingredients. Cover again and cook in the oven for 30 minutes, or until all the vegetables are tender.

Remove the bay leaf before serving.

Per serving: 111 Calories, 2g fat, 0g saturated fat, 0.1g sodium

Creamy hazelnut fettuccine with celery and soft herbs

Pasta and nuts have a great affinity, especially when used with fresh herbs, too. Other noodle-type pastas such as tagliatelle or pappardelle may be substituted for the fettuccine. **Serves 4**

½ cup whole blanched hazelnuts, lightly toasted

⅔ cup ricotta cheese

2 garlic cloves, crushed

1 teaspoon olive oil

1 shallot, finely chopped

2 stalks celery, peeled and finely diced

1 pound fresh or dried fettuccini

Freshly ground black pepper

Ground nutmeg

1 tablespoon roughly chopped flat-leaf parsley

1 tablespoon roughly chopped basil

Place the hazelnuts, cheese, and garlic in a blender and blitz to a smooth paste.

Heat the olive oil in a pan, add the shallot and celery and two tablespoons water, cover with a lid, and cook over low heat until the water is absorbed and vegetables have softened.

Cook the pasta in boiling water until *al dente* and season with pepper and nutmeg. Add the hazelnut sauce and toss well together, then add the parsley and basil, toss again and serve.

Per serving: 540 Calories, 15g fat, 4g saturated fat, 0.06g sodium

Saffron-roasted garlic gnocchis with fennel caponata

These gnocchi are a little time consuming, but worth it. Fresh saffron may be replaced with a little powdered saffron; the flavor is not as good, but it is cheaper and does the job. **Serves 4**

2 pounds floury potatoes, peeled and cut into chunks

Good pinch of saffron, dissolved in 1 tablespoon boiling water

1 teaspoon roasted garlic purée (see page 38)

Freshly ground black pepper

2½ cups all-purpose flour

1 egg

Handful basil leaves

For the caponata

1 tablespoon olive oil

2 fennel heads, cut into ½-inch dice

12 black olives, pitted and cut in half

2 tablespoons balsamic vinegar

3 ounces sun-blush tomatoes

½ teaspoon sugar

Place the potatoes in a pan, cover with water, and bring to a boil. Cook until tender, drain well, then return to the pan and dry over low heat.

Put the potatoes through a fine strainer or vegetable mill. Add the saffron, water, and garlic purée. Season with black pepper and mix well.

Add the flour and egg, then mix to a smooth dough. Using floured hands, roll the dough into a three-quarter inch cylinder, then cut into three-quarter inch lengths. With a fork, make a classic gnocchi indentation on each piece. Place the rolled gnocchi on a floured tray until ready to cook.

To make the caponata, heat the oil in a pan, add the fennel with two tablespoons water, cover, and cook until the fennel is tender and the water has evaporated.

Add the olives, vinegar, tomatoes, and sugar, cook for a further 10 minutes, season with black pepper to taste, and keep warm.

Cook the gnocchi in a pan of boiling water until they rise to the surface, then remove with a slotted spoon and drain well.

Dress the gnocchi with the fennel caponata, sprinkle the torn basil leaves on top, and serve.

Per serving: 498 Calories, 7g fat, 1g saturated fat, 0.47g sodium

Summer vegetable tagliatelle with lemon and tarragon

It is as easy to buy fresh pasta as dried, although nowadays the quality of dried pasta is excellent. This dish is also great served cold, tossed with a spoonful or two of vinaigrette. **Serves 4**

Juice of ½ lemon
1 tablespoon olive oil
1 teaspoon honey
2 scallions, finely chopped
2 tablespoons roughly chopped tarragon
7 ounces asparagus (about 8-10 spears)

4 ounces baby zucchini, cut into thick slices (about ¾ cup)
½ cup fresh or frozen peas
1 pound, 2 ounces fresh or 1 pound dried tagliatelle (or fettuccine)
12 sun-blush tomatoes
Freshly ground black pepper

Prepare a light lemon dressing by whisking together in a bowl the lemon juice, olive oil, honey, scallions, and tarragon.

Break off the woody end stems of the asparagus and, using a potato peeler, carefully peel the tips. Cut into one-inch lengths.

Cook the asparagus for two minutes in boiling water, then remove with a slotted spoon and quickly refresh in cold water.

Cook the zucchini in the boiling water for one minute, remove, and quickly refresh in cold water. Add the peas to the boiling water and cook for two to three minutes, remove, and quickly refresh.

Cook the fresh pasta in plenty of boiling water for two to three minutes until *al dente* (dried pasta will need a little longer–check package instructions). Drain the pasta, reserving a quarter cup of the cooking water, then return the pasta to the pan, add the drained asparagus, zucchini, and peas, along with the tomatoes, and toss well.

Add the lemon dressing and reserved pasta water, season with black pepper to taste, toss well together, and serve.

Per serving: 420 Calories, 7g fat, 1g saturated fat, 0.16g sodium

Casarecce pasta with grilled red peppers and peas

Casarecce is a hand-rolled pasta that has been formed in a twist. It is available from Italian delicatessens. Other tubular or twisted varieties can also be used, of course. **Serves 4**

2 tablespoons olive oil
2 large red peppers
1 cup fresh or frozen peas
1 pound dried casarecce pasta

5 tablespoons half-fat crème fraîche (or half-fat sour cream)
2 tablespoons chopped basil
Freshly ground black pepper

Preheat the broiler pan until hot, then brush the surface with a tablespoon of the oil. Broil the red peppers for 8–10 minutes until charred all over. Remove the peppers and place in a plastic bag for two to three minutes until the skins loosen, then remove from the bag, peel, remove membranes and seeds, and cut into wide strips.

Cook the peas in boiling water for two minutes until tender, refresh in cold water, drain, and dry well.

Cook the pasta in plenty of boiling water for 10–12 minutes until *al dente*. Drain well.

While the pasta is cooking, heat the remaining oil in a non-stick frying pan, add the pepper strips and crème fraîche, and cook for one minute. Add the peas, basil, and pasta, and toss the lot together. Season with black pepper to taste and serve immediately.

Per serving: 518 Calories, 11g fat, 3g saturated fat, 0.04g sodium

Eggplant, green olive, and preserved lemon risotto

This is a vegetarian risotto with a Moroccan feel. Although there are many types of risotto rice, I prefer Vialamo Namo. It has a great flavor, and low starch content, which keeps the grains firm and moist. **Serves 4**

1 tablespoon olive oil
1 eggplant, cut into 1-inch cubes, and blanched
1 onion, finely chopped
1 cup Vialamo Namo risotto rice
3 cups hot vegetable stock (see page 39)

12 plump green olives, pitted
1 tablespoon finely chopped preserved lemon
2 tablespoons roughly chopped flat-leaf parsley
Freshly ground black pepper

Heat the oil in a large non-stick pan. When hot, add the eggplant and onion, and fry for four to five minutes, until they are lightly browned.

Add the rice and stir to mix, along with the vegetables. Add the vegetable stock, a ladleful at a time, stirring constantly until each amount is absorbed before adding more, until all the stock is used up. Cook for 20–25 minutes.

Add the olives, lemon, and parsley, season with pepper to taste, and serve.

Should you have any risotto left over, it makes a great salad, tossed with a little low-fat vinaigrette.

Per serving: 237 Calories, 6g fat, 1g saturated fat, 0.5g sodium

Oven-baked pumpkin risotto

A recipe for a risotto that does away with the boredom of the continual stirring usually needed for risottos. Once it is in the oven, simply leave it to cook while you attend to other things. Pumpkin is very popular at the moment and contains lots of beta-carotene. **Serves 4**

1 pound pumpkin, peeled and cut into ½-inch dice
1 small onion, finely chopped
1 garlic clove, crushed
Oil-water spray (see page 33)
Freshly ground black pepper

1 cup Vialamo Namo risotto rice
Peel of ½ lemon
3 cups hot vegetable stock (see page 39)
1 ounce finely grated Parmesan cheese

Preheat the oven to 400°F.

Place the pumpkin, onion, and garlic in a non-stick ovenproof casserole dish. Spray the vegetables lightly with the oil-water spray and season lightly with black pepper.

Place in the oven for 15–20 minutes, until golden and caramelized, turning regularly.

Sprinkle the rice and lemon peel over them, and stir it all together. Pour in the boiling stock and stir well.

Cover with foil and return to the oven for 25–30 minutes or until the rice is tender and all the stock is absorbed.

Stir in half of the Parmesan, and scatter the remainder over the top and serve immediately.

Per serving: 228 Calories, 3g fat, 2g saturated fat, 0.31g sodium

Almond-crumbed fish with baked oven fries and cumin ketchup

We all love fish and chips, but they contain a lot of fat traditionally, so here is my low-fat recipe. Panko crumbs are coarse Japanese bread crumbs and can be found in from Oriental grocery stores. **Serves** 4

For the fish
¾ cup panko crumbs or bread crumbs
⅓ cup cut-up almonds
½ teaspoon ground cumin
½ teaspoon ground coriander
¼ teaspoon smoked paprika
Pinch of ground turmeric
Freshly ground black pepper
4 x 6-ounce cleaned halibut fillets, each cut into 2 finger-sized pieces
6 tablespoons all-purpose flour

2 egg whites, lightly beaten
Oil-water spray (see page 33)
1 lemon, sliced, for garnishing

For the fries
1¼ pounds baking potatoes
1 teaspoon unsaturated oil
1 large egg white, lightly beaten

For the cumin ketchup
2 tablespoons low-fat plain yogurt
½ teaspoon ground cumin
½ cup tomato ketchup

Preheat the oven to 400°F.

To make the fries, cut the washed potatoes into equal-sized wedges, dry them well, then dip in the egg white until they are thoroughly coated. Place in a non-stick baking pan, skin side down, and bake for 40–45 minutes until cooked and golden brown.

Combine the panko crumbs, almonds, and spices, together in a bowl with a little pepper.

Season the fish, then dredge with flour before coating them with the beaten egg whites, then dip them into the spiced crumb mix to coat.

Lightly spray the fish with a little oil-water spray, then place in a large non-stick baking pan.

Place in the oven to cook until golden, this should take about five to six minutes, depending on the thickness of your fish.

To make the cumin ketchup, mix all the ingredients in a bowl and season with black pepper to taste. Serve the fish and chips with the ketchup and some lemon slices for garnishing.

Per serving: 530 Calories, 13g fat, 1g saturated fat, 0.69g sodium

Grilled halibut with artichokes, potatoes, and chile parsley sauce

Grilling fish is the perfect way to keep fat to a minimum. Halibut is a fine fish for grilling, tender and juicy, and great for summer barbecues. **Serves** 4

11 ounces large new potatoes (probably less than 2)
Oil-water spray (see page 33)
One 14-ounce jar artichokes in water, drained and cut in half
1 tablespoon superfine capers, drained and rinsed
4 x 6-ounce thick halibut fillets, skinned

For the sauce
½ teaspoon Dijon mustard
½ small green chile, seeded and finely chopped
Juice of ½ lemon
1 teaspoon balsamic vinegar
1 teaspoon olive oil
2 canned anchovy fillets, rinsed and finely chopped
2 tablespoons roughly chopped parsley
Freshly ground black pepper

Wash the potatoes well, removing all dirt. Place in a pan of boiling water and cook for 15–20 minutes or until just tender, then refresh under cold water, and drain well. Cut the potatoes in half lengthwise and set aside.

To make the sauce, place the mustard and green chile, lemon juice, and balsamic vinegar in a bowl and mix together. Gradually add the oil, anchovies, a half-cup water, and the chopped parsley. Mix well together and season to taste with black pepper.

Heat a ridged grill pan over high heat, squirt with a little oil-water spray, then add the potatoes. Cook for five to six minutes, turning then regularly during cooking, until golden and slightly charred all over. Remove and keep warm. Do the same with the artichokes, then toss together with the potatoes and capers. Keep warm.

Season the halibut fillets, squirt with a little oil-water spray and grill for two to three minutes on each side.

Place the vegetables on four serving plates, top with a grilled halibut fillet, pour a little sauce over them, and serve.

Per serving: 263 Calories, 5g fat, 1g saturated fat, 0.39g sodium

Baked mustard cod with lemon peel and capers

A variation on a dish first prepared during my early days in the business, while working at the Royal Garden in London. I have never forgotten it, so I include it here for posterity. **Serves 4**

Oil-water spray (see page 33)
1 teaspoon Dijon mustard
4 x 6-ounce thick cod fillets, skinned
4 tomatoes
2 zucchini
Juice and peel of ½ lemon

1 tablespoon superfine capers, drained and rinsed
¼ cup dry white wine
⅔ cup fish stock (see page 39)
½ teaspoon freshly-picked thyme leaves
1 tablespoon roughly chopped fresh tarragon

Preheat the oven to 400°F.

Lightly grease a large non-stick baking tray with the oil-water spray. Brush the mustard lightly over the surface of each fish fillet and place on the tray.

Slice the tomatoes and zucchini into half-inch thick slices. Blanch the zucchini in boiling water for one minute, drain, refresh in a bowl of cold water, and dry them. Lay overlapping slices of tomato and zucchini on each fish fillet, alternating them for color. Sprinkle a little lemon peel and a few capers over each fillet.

Pour the white wine, fish stock, and lemon juice, and sprinkle the thyme and tarragon on top.

Loosely cover the tray with foil to secure the juices, and bake in the oven until cooked through, this will take about five to eight minutes depending on the thickness of the cod.

When the fish is cooked, remove carefully to serving dishes. Strain any cooking juices and pour any remaining juices over the fish before serving.

Per serving: 187 Calories, 2g fat, 0g saturated fat, 0.31g sodium

Pan-caramelized cod with sweet-and-sour shallots

Cod is a very delicate fish and can be prepared in all sorts of ways, from baking or poaching to frying and braising, as in my recipe here with sweet-and-sour shallots and ginger. **Serves 4**

12 Thai shallots, peeled
¼ cup reduced-salt light soy sauce
2 tablespoons brown sugar
¼ cup white wine vinegar
1 x 2-inch piece of fresh ginger root, peeled and very finely chopped

1 teaspoon coriander seeds
¼ teaspoon freshly ground black pepper
4 x 6-ounce cod fillets, skinned
⅓ cup dry white wine
1 cup fish stock (see page 39)
⅓ cup orange juice
1 tablespoon finely chopped chives

Preheat the oven to 400°F.

Peel the shallots and cook in a pan of boiling water for three to four minutes. Remove with a slotted spoon and refresh in cold water, then dry them well.

In a large non-stick ovenproof pan, heat a little of the soy sauce with the sugar and vinegar and bring to a boil. Add the ginger root, coriander seeds, and black pepper, and cook until the liquid caramelizes lightly into a syrup.

Season the cod fillets with a little pepper, then add to the syrup. Cook for two minutes until the fish begins to caramelize, then turn the fillets over with a spatula.

Pour over the white wine, fish stock, and orange juice, then tuck in the shallots around the fish. Cover with a lid and place in the oven for four to five minutes or until the fish is cooked.

Remove the fish carefully from the pan onto serving plates, top with the shallots, and pour the sauce over the fish. If the sauce is too thin, pour it into a pan, and, over a high heat, reduce it down to a syrup-like consistency that coats the back of a spoon. Sprinkle the chives on top and serve with a sweet potato mash made with finely chopped red chiles and, of course, skim milk.

Per serving: 210 Calories, 2g fat, 0g saturated fat, 0.89g sodium

Steamed sea bass with ginger and sweet chili
Sea bass is the king of fish and is usually expensive, but superb for that special dinner party treat. Trout or salmon could easily be used instead, however, with equal success.

Serves 4

Handful of fresh seaweed (optional)
1-inch piece of fresh ginger root, peeled and finely chopped, peels retained
2 star anis
4 x 6-ounce thick sea bass fillets, skinned
½ lemongrass stalk, very finely chopped

For the broth
4 scallions, cut in 1-inch lengths

8 shiitake mushrooms, sliced
⅔ cup chicken stock (see page 39)
1 garlic clove, crushed
2 tablespoons dry sherry
1 tablespoon reduced-salt soy sauce
2 tablespoons sweet chilli sauce
1 teaspoon sesame oil
2 tablespoons roughly shredded holy basil

Place the seaweed, ginger peels, and star anis in a pan large enough to hold a bamboo steamer on top. Cover with 300ml one and a quarter cups water, bring to a boil, and simmer for two to three minutes.

Place the sea bass fillets in the bamboo steamer and scatter the finely chopped ginger and lemongrass on top. Cover with a lid, place the steamer over the pan, and steam for five minutes.

Meanwhile, prepare the broth. Put all the ingredients in a pan and bring to a boil, then simmer for two to three minutes, to meld the flavors.

Place the fish in deep serving bowls, pour the broth in and serve with steamed rice and oriental greens such as bok choy or Chinese broccoli.

Per serving: 212 Calories, 5g fat, 1g saturated fat, 0.57g sodium

Cod with sweet pepper and portabello bolognese
For me, cod is one of the greatest and most versatile of fish: it poaches, bakes, and deep-fries well, and can take lots of diverse flavors to accompany it. This spicy pepper and mushroom sauce is a great example. **Serves 4**

Oil-water spray (see page 33)
1 onion, finely diced
1 garlic clove, crushed
1 carrot, finely diced
2 ounces chorizo sausage, finely diced (about ½ cup)
1 red pepper, roasted, skinned, seeded, and finely chopped
2 Portobello mushrooms, peeled and finely chopped
1 tablespoon thyme leaves

7 ounces canned tomatoes, chopped (¾ cup)
1 teaspoon tomato paste
1 tablespoon brown sugar
¼ cup red wine
1 teaspoon Worcestershire sauce
4 x 6-ounce cod fillets, skinned
Freshly ground black pepper
Pinch of paprika

To make the bolognese sauce, add a squirt of oil-water spray to a non-stick frying pan and heat. Add the onion, garlic, and carrot, and two teaspoons water, and cover with a lid. Cook for about five minutes until the vegetables begin to soften, stirring regularly.

Add the chorizo, red pepper, Portobello mushrooms, and thyme, and cook for a further five minutes. Add the tomatoes, tomato paste, brown sugar, red wine, and Worcestershire sauce, and simmer for 20 minutes over medium heat.

Heat another non-stick frying pan with a squirt of oil-water spray. Season the cod fillets with black pepper and a pinch of paprika and cook for three to four minutes on each side, until golden and crispy. Remove from the pan and serve with the bolognese sauce on a bed of fresh noodles.

Per serving: 251 Calories, 5g fat, 1g saturated fat, 0.25g sodium

Hake with shellfish in green butter

Don't panic! The green butter isn't butter at all; it's the name given to the rich garlicky herb paste, which is so delicious and buttery in taste, but without the fat, of course. Cod may be substituted for hake, if it is more readily available. **Serves 4**

Oil-water spray (see page 33)
4 x 6-ounce hake steaks
Freshly ground black pepper
9 ounces mussels, cleaned and
    beards removed
9 ounces baby clams, washed

2½ cups hot fish stock (see
    page 39)

For the green butter
3 garlic cloves, crushed
1 canned anchovy fillet,
    drained and rinsed
Handful of flat-leaf parsley

To make the green butter, blitz the garlic, anchovy, and parsley to a smooth paste in a blender. Place in a bowl, cover, and keep in the fridge.

Lightly spray a large flameproof casserole dish or other heavy pan with the oil-water spray. Season the hake steaks with pepper and place in the pan.

Scatter the cleaned mussels and clams over the fish, then pour in the hot fish stock. Bring to a boil over high heat, cover with a lid, reduce the heat, and cook for four to five minutes, until the fish is cooked and tender and the shellfish have opened.

Remove the fish and shellfish to four serving bowls.

Return the casserole to the heat and whisk in the "butter", season to taste, then pour it over the fish and serve.

Per serving: 200 Calories, 5g fat, 1g saturated fat, 0.48g sodium

Bajan snapper

Marinating fish is one of the easiest ways to give it flavor, while the chilled dressing is the perfect foil for the spicy foods with which it is served. Mojos (pronounced "Mohos") are served all over the Caribbean islands with charcoal-grilled foods, such as fish and meats. **Serves 4**

4 x 6-ounce skinless, cleaned
    snapper fillets
4 scallions
1 green pepper, seeded and
    chopped
1 stalk celery, peeled and
    chopped
1 red chile, stem removed and
    chopped
1 tablespoon picked thyme
    leaves
1 tablespoon marjoram leaves
¼ cup chopped flat-leaf
    parsley
Juice of 2 limes

4 garlic cloves, peeled
Freshly ground black pepper
Oil-water spray (see page 33)
For the mojo dressing
1 mango, peeled and cut into
    ½-inch dice
1 red onion, chopped
3 plum tomatoes, seeded and
    cut into ½-inch dice
1 garlic clove, crushed
Juice of 2 limes
2 tablespoons roughly
    chopped mint
1 teaspoon sugar

Preheat the oven to 450°F.

To make the bajan paste, place the scallions in a blender along with the remaining ingredients, except the snapper fillets and the oil, and blitz to a paste.

Place the snapper fillet in a shallow dish and rub the paste all over both sides of the fish, cover with plastic wrap and let marinate for a minimum of two hours at room temperature.

To make the mojo dressing, place all the ingredients in a bowl and marinate for 30 minutes.

Remove any excess marinade from around the snapper fillets and place them on a large non-stick baking tray that's been greased with a little oil-water spray. Place in the oven for eight to nine minutes until cooked.

Dress with the mojo dressing and serve on a bed of steamed white rice with some grilled pumpkin or squash.

Per serving: 250 Calories, 3g fat, 0g saturated fat, 0.15g sodium

Pan-grilled tuna with Swiss chard, Moroccan salsa

Fresh tuna is now becoming more widely available, which is terrific since it is a beautiful, meaty fish, rich in omega-3. To appreciate tuna at its best, it should be lightly cooked, otherwise it becomes dry and loses its texture. **Serves 4**

1 tablespoon olive oil
½ teaspoon ground cumin
⅛ teaspoon ground turmeric
½ teaspoon ground cinnamon
2 roasted red peppers, peeled, seeded and cut into ¼-inch dice
2 tomatoes, blanched, seeded and cut into ¼-inch dice
12 black olives, pitted
½ cup tomato juice
½ teaspoon cayenne
1 garlic clove, crushed
2 tablespoons roughly chopped cilantro
2 tablespoons roughly chopped mint
½ cup fresh dates, pitted, peeled, and cut into ¼-inch dice
Juice and peel of ½ orange
Juice of ½ lemon
Freshly ground black pepper
14 ounces Swiss chard, leaves only
4 x 6-ounce thick tuna fillet steaks

Heat half of the oil in a non-stick pan over medium heat, then add the cumin, turmeric, and cinnamon, and let it infuse for 30 seconds. Add the red peppers, tomatoes, olives, and tomato juice, and cook for a further two minutes. Add everything else, except the remaining oil, the chard, and tuna. Season with black pepper to taste, and keep warm.

Cook the chard for two to three minutes in a pan of boiling water, then remove and drain well. (Alternatively, steam the chard in a colander over a pan of boiling water.)

Heat a ridged grill pan until it is almost smoking, then brush with the remaining oil. Season the tuna fillets and cook for one to two minutes on each side until charred on the outside, while the center remains slightly pink.

Serve the tuna steaks on a bed of chard, spoon the salsa over them, and serve. In keeping with the flavor of Morocco, fluffy steamed couscous would make an excellent accompaniment.

Per serving: 354 Calories, 13g fat, 3g saturated fat, 0.51g sodium

Smoked chili shrimp with fennel and beet tzatziki

Tzatziki is a Greek salad made with cucumber and yogurt. Here I use beets, which have a sweet flavor to balance the yogurt. They have a wonderful color, too, and make a refreshing contrast for the spicy shrimp. **Serves 4**

1 large head fennel
½ cup rice wine or white wine vinegar
3 tablespoons sugar
1 teaspoon smoked paprika
¼ teaspoon chili powder
16 large tiger shrimp, shelled and deveined
2 tablespoons chopped dill, plus whole leaves for garnishing
4 lemon wedges, for garnishing

For the beet tzatziki
½ cup low-fat plain yogurt
2 medium beets, cooked and shredded
1 garlic clove, crushed
1 tablespoon red wine vinegar
1 tablespoon olive oil
Freshly ground black pepper

Using a kitchen mandoline set at its thinnest setting, slice the fennel, then place in a bowl.

Heat the rice wine and sugar in a pan over low heat until the sugar has dissolved. Pour the hot vinegar over the fennel, cover with plastic wrap and set aside to marinate for one hour.

In another bowl, mix the paprika and chili powder, then rub the shrimp all over with the spice mix.

To make the tzatziki, mix the yogurt, shredded beets, and garlic in a bowl. Stir in the vinegar and olive oil, then season with black pepper.

Heat a non-stick frying pan and, when hot, dry-fry the shrimp, turning them constantly until cooked and slightly charred all over, this should take about two to three minutes.

Drain the fennel and toss with the chopped dill.

To serve, divide the fennel between four plates, top with some beet tzatziki, then the shrimp. Garnish with the dill leaves and lemon wedges.

Per serving: 202 Calories, 4g fat, 1g saturated fat, 0.29g sodium

"Baked trout in the news" *The idea of cooking fish in newspaper came while on a trip to Scotland, salmon fishing for the* Sunday Telegraph *ten years ago. The gillie, John Burrow, showed us how to cook our catch on an open fire. Using the oven is fine for retaining the flavors.* **Serves 4**

4½ pounds trout or salmon, gutted and scaled (ask your fishmonger to do this)
Freshly ground black pepper
¼ cup half-fat crème fraîche or half-fat sour cream
4 sheets newspaper
1 sheet parchment paper
Oil-water spray (see page 33)
¼ cup fresh dill
½ lemon, thinly sliced
¼ cup Pernod (or other anise-style liqueur)

Preheat the oven to 400°F.

Dry the inside cavity of the trout with paper towels and season with black pepper.

Place the newspaper and parchment paper under running water until they are wet.

Lay the newspaper sheets on top of each other on a flat surface, top with the wet sheet of parchment, and spray with a little oil-water spray. Place the trout in the center of the paper, pour the crème fraîche over it, and sprinkle liberally with the dill. Scatter the lemon slices over the fish, then pour the Pernod over it.

Carefully wrap up the fish in the paper, tucking in the end to enclose the fish completely. Place on a baking sheet and bake in the oven for 30–40 minutes or until the wet paper is dry – an indicator that the fish is cooked.

Unwrap in front of your guests and cut into portions. Serve with zucchini, almonds, and new potatoes.

Per serving: 373 Calories, 13g fat, 4g saturated fat, 0.17g sodium

Miso ginger steamed salmon *I make no excuses for the strong Asian emphasis in this section of the book. I have a great love of this cuisine: delicate yet robust flavors that are low in fat, but high in taste. Miso paste can be bought from Oriental grocery stores or healthfood stores.* **Serves 4**

1 tablespoon red miso paste
1 teaspoon unsaturated oil
2 tablespoons ketchap manis (Indonesian soy sauce)
2-inch piece of fresh ginger root, peeled and very finely chopped
1 tablespoon rice wine vinegar
1 tablespoon honey
4 x 6-ounce fresh salmon fillets, skinned
2 small bok choy, cut in half lengthwise
5 ounces shiitake mushrooms, cut in half (2-2½ cups)
6 scallions, peeled and cut into 1-inch lengths
Freshly ground black pepper

In a bowl, whisk the miso paste with the oil, half the soy sauce, and the ginger. Pour in the rice wine vinegar and honey, and stir well together.

Place the salmon fillets in a shallow dish, pour the miso mixture over them, and turn the fillets until well coated. Cover with plastic wrap and place in the fridge for one hour.

Remove the salmon fillets from the marinade and wipe off any excess; discard the marinade. Place the fillets flat in a steamer basket, cover with the lid, and place over a pan of boiling water. Cook for three to four minutes or until just tender.

At the same time, using another basket, steam the bok choy, mushrooms, and scallions for three to four minutes until cooked. Remove from the heat and season with black pepper.

Serve the steamed vegetables topped with a steamed salmon fillet and drizzle the remaining soy sauce around them.

Per serving: 354 Calories, 20g fat, 4g saturated fat, 0.8g sodium

Salmon arrancini with tomato and cucumber dressing

Arrancini is the Italian term given to small orange-shaped balls made of rice with fish or meat, then deep-fried. Canned salmon is ideal and is full of goodness. Bake or broil with equally successful results. **Serves 4**

1 cup dry risotto rice, then cooked

1 egg, hard-boiled and roughly chopped

One 7½-ounce can red salmon, drained and flaked

1 tablespoon chopped fresh basil

1 tablespoon chopped fresh parsley

Freshly ground black pepper

1 egg white, beaten

3 cups fresh white breadcrumbs

1 lemon, sliced, for garnishing

Salad greens, for garnishing

For the dressing

½ cup low-fat plain yogurt

2 tablespoons chopped fresh basil

4 tomatoes, cut into ½-inch cubes (about ⅔ cup)

4 ounces cucumber, cut into ½-inch cubes (about ⅔ cup)

Place the cooked rice in a bowl, add the egg, salmon, and chopped herbs, and season with black pepper. Place the mixture in the refrigerator for one hour to chill.

Preheat the oven to 375°F.

Remove the mixture from the refrigerator and shape into small balls about one and a half inches in diameter. Roll them through the beaten egg white, and then in the breadcrumbs, coating the balls evenly.

Arrange the arrancini on a non-stick baking sheet and place in the oven to cook for 10–25 minutes, until crisp and golden, or alternatively cook them under a hot broiler, turning them occasionally.

To make the dressing, mix together the yogurt and basil, add the tomatoes and cucumber, and season with black pepper.

Drizzle the dressing over the arrancini and garnish with lemon and salad greens. This dish is also great served with steamed new potatoes and green beans.

Per serving: 427 Calories, 7g fat, 1g saturated fat, 0.52g sodium

Monkfish biryani

Monkfish is a very forgiving fish, and certainly responds well to forceful treatment. It is particularly good for robust hearty dishes, combined with spices and herbs, such as this Indian-style biryani dish. Serve with yogurt and rice for a great meal. **Serves 4**

2 cups basmati rice

2 teaspoons unsaturated oil

1½ pounds monkfish fillet, cleaned

1 onion, sliced

1-inch piece of fresh ginger root, finely chopped

2 garlic cloves, crushed

1 teaspoon ground coriander

½ teaspoon cumin seeds

1 teaspoon ground turmeric

½ teaspoon chili powder

7 ounces cauliflower, cut into florets (about 1 cup)

4 tomatoes, peeled and quartered

¼ cup golden raisins

1 teaspoon garam masala

2 eggs, hard-boiled and quartered

¾ cup cashews

Cilantro, for garnishing

Place the rice in a strainer and rinse under cold running water until the water runs clear, then put the rice in a saucepan with 3 cups water. Bring to a boil, reduce the heat, and simmer for 10 minutes or until the rice is tender. Drain well.

Heat one teaspoon of the oil in a heavy saucepan over high heat. Add the monkfish fillet and seal for one to two minutes until golden all over, then set aside. Add the remaining oil, the onion, ginger, and garlic, and cook for one minute. Add the coriander, cumin, turmeric, and chili powder, and fry for two minutes, stirring constantly to prevent the spices from catching on the pan and burning.

Add two and a half cups water to the spiced onion mixture and bring to a boil. Add the cauliflower, tomatoes, and raisins, and simmer for 15 minutes. Add the rice, return the fish to the pan, stir in the garam masala, and simmer for two to three minutes to let the flavours develop and finish cooking the fish. Serve garnished with the egg, cashews and cilantro.

Per serving: 665 Calories, 16g fat, 2g saturated fat, 0.1g sodium

Charbroiled mackerel with tomato chutney and braised fennel

This chutney is a real winner, but is best made about one month in advance, to let the flavors come through. Mackerel is full of good omega-3 fatty acids, hence the fat content of this recipe. **Serves 4**

2 large heads of fennel, peeled and thickly sliced
Peel of ¼ lemon
1¼ cups chicken stock (see page 39)
Freshly ground black pepper
1 tablespoon olive oil
1 garlic clove, crushed
Juice of ½ lemon
1 teaspoon smoked paprika
4 x 5½-ounce mackerel fillets

For the tomato chutney
⅔ cup red wine vinegar
⅓ cup brown sugar
½ teaspoon dried chili flakes
¼ cup raisins
1 small onion, chopped
1 Granny Smith apple, peeled and chopped
One 14½-ounce can tomatoes, finely chopped
Pinch each of cayenne and ground cinnamon

Preheat the oven to 400°F.

To make the chutney, place the vinegar, sugar, spices, and raisins in a pan and bring to a boil, stirring until the sugar dissolves. Reduce the heat, add the onion, apple, and tomatoes, and simmer gently for 30 minutes until the mixture is thick. Season to taste with cayenne and cinnamon and let cool completely.

Place the fennel on a roasting tray, add the lemon peel, pour the stock in, and season with black pepper to taste. Cover with foil and bake in the oven until tender, this should take about 30 minutes.

Place the olive oil, garlic, lemon juice, and smoked paprika in a dish, season the mackerel with black pepper, and place in the marinade for 20 minutes.

Grill the fish on a barbecue or grill pan or under a hot broiler until cooked and slightly charred.

Serve the grilled mackerel on a bed of braised fennel with some tomato chutney.

Per serving: 535 Calories, 29g fat, 5g saturated fat, 0.31g sodium

Mackerel tagine

Tagine, which means stew, is a staple of Moroccan cuisine and is traditionally cooked in an earthenware dish with a pointed lid. Made with meat, vegetables, or fish, tagines are easy to prepare and are always flavorful and impressive. **Serves 4**

Oil-water spray (see page 33)
1 onion, finely chopped
2 garlic cloves, crushed
¼ teaspoon fennel seeds
½ teaspoon ground cinnamon
¼ teaspoon smoked paprika
½ teaspoon dried chili flakes
1 teaspoon ground cumin
½ teaspoon ground coriander
¼ teaspoon ground turmeric
1 small bay leaf
2 tablespoons golden raisins

One 14½-ounce can tomatoes
1 teaspoon tomato paste
1 teaspoon harissa paste (hot spice paste)
2 cups fish stock (see page 39)
One 15-ounce can chickpeas, drained and rinsed
12 black olives, pitted
Freshly ground black pepper
1½ pounds mackerel fillets
Sprigs of fresh cilantro, for garnishing

Heat a non-stick frying pan with a little oil-water spray. Add the onion, garlic, fennel seeds, and two tablespoons water, cover and sauté until the vegetables are soft, this should take about six to eight minutes.

Add all the spices, the bay leaf, and raisins, and cook uncovered for two to three minutes to let the spices release their fragrance.

Add the tomatoes, tomato paste, and harissa paste, with the fish stock, and bring to a boil. Cook over medium heat until the sauce reduces and thickens in consistency. Add the chickpeas and olives.

Season with black pepper, then carefully lay the mackerel fillets on top. Cover with a lid and simmer over gentle heat for six to eight minutes or until the mackerel is cooked through.

Place the fish on serving plates, pour the sauce over it, sprinkle with the fresh cilantro, and serve.

Per serving: 539 Calories, 32g fat, 5g saturated fat, 0.66g sodium

Linguine with anchovy olivada, tomatoes, and capers

A pasta so simple to prepare, I am sometimes embarrassed to give the recipe, but oh, what flavor! Try it and see for yourself what I mean. It can also be made with sardines. **Serves 4**

1 teaspoon olive oil
2 shallots, finely chopped
1 garlic clove, crushed
8 salted anchovy fillets, rinsed, drained, and finely chopped
8 black olives, pitted and finely chopped
4 ounces sun-blush tomatoes, drained and roughly chopped
1 pound, 2 ounces fresh or dried linguine pasta
1 tablespoon superfine capers, rinsed and drained
2 tablespoons roughly chopped flat-leaf parsley

Heat the oil in a non-stick pan, add the shallots and garlic, and cook over low heat for one minute.

Add the anchovies, olives, and tomatoes, and heat gently over low heat.

Cook the pasta in plenty of boiling water until *al dente*, then drain, reserving a quarter cup of the pasta water.

Add the drained pasta and reserved water to the anchovy mixture, then add the capers and parsley. Toss well together and serve in deep pasta bowls.

Per serving: 496 Calories, 5g fat, 1g saturated fat, 0.72g sodium

Baked smoked haddock pasta

Smoked haddock is a great fish, very flavorful and fairly inexpensive. Always buy natural smoked haddock rather than the yellow dried variety. This is real comfort food, but without the calories. **Serves 4**

4 strips lean bacon
11 ounces bucatini pasta
1 cup skim milk
12 ounces smoked haddock fillet, skinned
1 egg yolk
2 egg whites
3 tablespoons half-fat crème fraîche (or half-fat sour cream)
2 teaspoons Dijon mustard
2 tablespoons half-fat Cheddar cheese
Freshly ground black pepper

Preheat the oven to 375°F.

Place the bacon on a non-stick baking tray and cook for 10 minutes until lightly crisp, then remove and roughly chop into pieces. Cook the pasta in boiling water until *al dente*, and drain well.

In a pan, bring the milk to a boil. Lower the heat, add the smoked haddock, and poach for three to four minutes. Remove the fish with a slotted spoon and, when cool, lightly flake it, then strain the milk.

Pour the cooking milk into a bowl, and let it cool slightly. Add the eggs, crème fraîche, the mustard, and half the Cheddar, then season to taste with black pepper.

Add the fish and bacon to the cream mix and combine well together. Place the bucatini in an ovenproof baking dish, pour the smoked haddock and bacon cream over it, toss together, and scatter the remaining Cheddar on top. Bake for 20–25 minutes until set and the top is bubbling and golden.

Per serving: 451 Calories, 8g fat, 3g saturated fat, 1.32g sodium

Thai chicken bitoks

Bitoks are the name given to small burger-type patties. These bitoks may be prepared a day in advance, but if you do so, only top with the marinade for two hours before you want to serve. A simple but flavorsome dish, great for snacking as well. **Serves 4**

1 pound lean chicken breasts, ground up	**For the marinade**
2 egg whites, lightly beaten	2 tablespoons chopped cilantro
2 scallions, chopped	½-inch piece of fresh ginger root, grated
1 tablespoon ketchap manis (Indonesian soy sauce)	1 garlic clove, crushed
1-inch piece of fresh ginger root, finely chopped	½ teaspoon sweet chili sauce
1 tablespoon chopped cilantro	½ teaspoon ground turmeric
Freshly ground black pepper	1 tablespoon peanut oil
	1 tablespoon rice wine or white wine vinegar

In a bowl, combine the ground chicken with the egg whites, scallions, soy sauce, ginger, and cilantro. Season with a little pepper and mix together. Using wet hands, mold into eight small patties, about an inch thick.

Combine all the marinade ingredients together with a tablespoon of water in a bowl. Pour it over the patties, cover with plastic wrap and refrigerate for two hours.

Remove the patties from the marinade and place on a preheated broiler pan or on a baking tray under a traditional preheated broiler for five to six minutes, until cooked.

Serve with a traditional stir-fry of vegetables.

Per serving: 170 Calories, 4g fat, 1g saturated fat, 0.37g sodium

Oriental sticky braised chicken

I love this chicken dish with its sweet-and-sour Oriental flavors. The chicken is marinated, then cooked until the sauce becomes thick and sticky — one of those finger-licking recipes that just make your mouth water. **Serves 4**

4 large chicken legs, skin removed	3 tablespoons chopped fresh Thai basil leaves
2-inch piece of fresh ginger root, peeled, thinly sliced	2 tablespoons roasted cashews
½ cup dry sherry	Oil-water spray (see page 33)
4 star anis	**For the marinade**
2¼ cups chicken stock (see page 39)	2 lemongrass stalks, finely chopped
½ cup fresh or concentrated orange juice	1 small red chile, chopped
1 tablespoon tamarind paste	3 tablespoons ketchap manis (Indonesian soy sauce)
	1 tablespoon honey

To make the marinade, mix all the ingredients together in a large bowl. Add the chicken legs, mix well with the marinade, and leave for two hours at room temperature. Remove the chicken legs from the marinade. Set aside the marinade.

Squirt a little oil-water spray in a non-stick frying pan and heat. Add the chicken legs and cook for four to five minutes until golden, then remove from the pan.

Return the pan to the heat, add the ginger and sherry, and boil for two minutes. Add the marinade and all the remaining ingredients, except the Thai basil leaves and cashews.

Cook over high heat for five to six minutes, then return the chicken legs to the sauce. Cover with a lid and cook for a further 10 minutes until the sauce is reduced and sticky in consistency. Remove the star anis.

Remove the chicken legs to a serving dish and pour the sauce over them. Sprinkle with the Thai basil and cashews, and serve with white rice and stir-fried vegetables.

Per serving: 310 Calories, 7g fat, 2g saturated fat, 1.11g sodium

Cold chicken with tuna and black bean corn salsa

This dish is based on the Italian dish vitello tonnato, *poached veal set on a tuna sauce. Chicken makes a great and cheaper alternative, while the salsa gives the dish a little sparkle.* **Serves 4**

4 x 5-ounce chicken breasts, skinless

5 ounces canned tuna in water, drained (about ½ cup)

1 tablespoon superfine capers, rinsed and drained

½ garlic clove, crushed

½ cup reduced-calorie mayonnaise

Juice of ¼ lemon

Freshly ground black pepper

Handful of arugula

For the salsa

½ cup dried black beans, soaked overnight

½ cup frozen corn, defrosted

1 small red onion, chopped

½ garlic clove, crushed

Juice of ½ lemon

2 tablespoons maple syrup

1 tablespoon olive oil

Steam the chicken in a steamer over boiling water for 15–18 minutes, remove from heat, and let cool completely.

To make the salsa, drain the beans and place in a pan. Cover with water, bring to a boil, and simmer for 30–40 minutes or until soft. Drain and cool. Place in a bowl, add the remaining ingredients, and let infuse for 30 minutes.

Place the tuna, capers, and garlic in a blender and blitz to a purée. Transfer to a bowl and stir in the mayonnaise and lemon juice. Season with black pepper to taste.

To serve, slice the chicken into ¼-inch thick slices. Divide the tuna sauce between four plates and top with the sliced chicken. Toss the arugula in a little of the salsa juices and pile on top of the chicken.

Spoon the salsa over that, and serve with good crusty bread.

Per serving: 405 Calories, 14g fat, 3g saturated fat, 0.52g sodium

Deviled chicken paillard with lemon and cilantro couscous

Pomegranate molasses (also known as dibs Rumen*) is a staple of the Middle Eastern countries. It is wonderfully sweet and syrupy, well worth looking for in a Middle Eastern grocery store.* **Serves 4**

4 x 6-ounce chicken breasts, skinless

2 tablespoons whole-grain mustard

1 teaspoon Szechuan peppercorns, finely crushed

Juice and peel of ½ lemon

2 garlic cloves

1 tablespoon chopped oregano

1 tablespoon chopped cilantro

2 tablespoons pomegranate molasses

Oil-water spray (see page 33)

For the couscous

¾ cup couscous

1¼ cups hot chicken stock (see page 39)

⅓ cup currants, soaked in water and drained

2 tablespoons pine nuts

4 scallions, shredded

¼ cup cilantro

Freshly ground black pepper

Using the side of a meat cleaver, lightly bash the chicken to obtain a thick steak-like breast of uniform thickness.

In a bowl, mix the mustard, Szechuan pepper, lemon juice and zest, garlic, herbs, and molasses to form a light paste. Brush the chicken breasts all over with the paste and let marinate for one hour.

Preheat the broiler to its highest setting.

Place the couscous in a large bowl, pour the hot chicken stock over it, cover, and let stand for five to eight minutes. Fluff the couscous with a fork, then add the currants, pine nuts, scallions and cilantro, mix well, and season with black pepper to taste.

Lightly spray a baking sheet with the oil-water spray. Place the chicken breasts on it and cook under the broiler for six to eight minutes until golden.

Divide the couscous between four plates, place the chicken on top, and serve.

Per serving: 402 Calories, 7g fat, 1g saturated fat, 0.32g sodium

Pollo arrabbiato (spicy chicken stew with pumpkin, chile, and tomatoes)

A spicy chicken dish I love to prepare, though I have to admit that I use a lot more chile than in the recipe. Arrabbiato *is the name of the spicy tomato sauce popular in the Middle East.* **Serves 4**

Oil-water spray (see page 33)
9 ounces small pearl onions (about 2-2½ cups)
2 tablespoons brown sugar
9 ounces pumpkin, skin removed, cut into 1-inch dice (about 2-2½ cups)
2 garlic cloves, crushed
2 red chiles, seeded and finely chopped
3½ pounds chicken, cut into pieces, skin removed
Freshly ground black pepper
1 tablespoon balsamic vinegar
1 tablespoon oregano
½ cup dry white wine
One 14½-ounce can tomatoes, chopped

Preheat the oven to 400°F.

Heat a squirt of oil-water spray in a large flameproof casserole dish or other heavy ovenproof pan, then add the onions, cover, and fry until golden, this should take about 10 minutes. Remove the lid, add the brown sugar, and caramelize lightly. Add the pumpkin, garlic, and chiles, and cook for a further five minutes. Remove from the pan and set aside.

Season the chicken pieces with black pepper. Return the dish to the heat, add the chicken pieces, and cook until they begin to color, turning once or twice. Pour the vinegar over them, and cook for one minute. Return the vegetables to the pan, add the oregano, and raise the heat. Pour in the wine , cook for five minutes, then add the chopped tomatoes. Season with black pepper, cover with a lid, and place in the oven to cook for about 40–45 minutes or until the chicken is cooked and tender. Serve with soft polenta.

Per serving: 310 Calories, 5g fat, 1g saturated fat, 0.24g sodium

Posh coq au vin *A retro recipe based on a classic French dish, chicken in red wine is usually made with button mushrooms, but I've replaced them with the woody flavor of wild mushrooms. Dried wild mushrooms are now ready available, and need to be soaked before using.* **Serves 4**

Oil-water spray (see page 33)
4 large chicken legs, skinned and cut into thighs and drumsticks
1 tablespoon all-purpose flour
Freshly ground black pepper
5 ounces small pearl onions, peeled (about 1¼-1½ cups)
4 slices bacon, cut into strips
7 ounces mixed fresh wild mushrooms, cleaned, sliced (about 2 cups)
2 garlic cloves, crushed
⅔ cup good-quality red wine
1 tablespoon tomato paste
4 cups hot chicken stock (see page 39)
2 sprigs of fresh thyme
1 small bay leaf

Preheat the oven to 400°F.

Heat a squirt of oil-water spray in a large non-stick flameproof casserole dish or other heavy ovenproof pan. Dust the chicken pieces with the flour mixed with black pepper. Add to the pan and fry for four to five minutes on each side until the chicken is browned. Remove the chicken from the pan and place to one side.

Add the onions and bacon and cook for five minutes, until browned all over. Then add the wild mushrooms and garlic and cook for a further five minutes until the mushrooms are browned. Add the red wine and boil for two to three minutes.

Return the chicken to the pan, add the tomato paste, and carefully mix well. Add the stock a little at a time to form a sauce. Bring to a boil, tuck in the thyme and bay leaf, cover with a lid, and place in the oven to cook for 25–30 minutes or until the chicken is tender and the sauce reduced in consistency and intense in flavor.

Remove the thyme and bay leaf and serve with mashed potatoes and steamed spinach.

Per serving: 265 Calories, 7g fat, 2g saturated fat, 0.89g sodium

Stuffed chicken with dried fruits, almonds, and wild rice

An impressive chicken dish filled with dried fruits, nuts, and wild rice, instead of normal rice. In fact, wild rice is no relative of rice at all, but the grain of watergrass native to North America. **Serves 4**

¾ cup wild rice

4 x 6-ounce chicken breasts, skinless

2 ounces ready-to-eat dried fruits, in ¼-inch dice (about ¼ cup)

2 scallions, finely chopped

¼ cup cut-up almonds, toasted

2 tablespoons raisins, soaked in water until swollen, drained

1 teaspoon smoked paprika

Freshly ground black pepper

2 tablespoons low-fat fromage frais (or low-fat plain yogurt)

2 tablespoons cilantro

2 teaspoons unsaturated oil

For the corn and mustard salsa

½ cup canned corn

2 tomatoes, seeded and chopped

1 tablespoon chopped cilantro

Juice of 1 lime

1 teaspoon whole-grain mustard

1 tablespoon honey

1 garlic clove, crushed

Steam or boil the wild rice for 40–45 minutes until tender.

To make the salsa, heat a non-stick frying pan. Drain the corn, then dry-fry until golden for two to three minutes, tossing it in the pan occasionally. Tip into a bowl, add the remaining ingredients, and marinate for one hour.

Preheat the oven to 400°F.

Lay the chicken breasts on a counter and, using a sharp knife, cut a pocket into them along the length of the sides, ensuring that you don't cut right through.

Mix together the rice, fruits, onions, almonds, raisins, paprika, and pepper. Stir in the fromage frais and cilantro, then mix well. Open the pocket of each chicken and fill with the rice stuffing. Close the pocket and secure with two toothpicks.

Heat the oil in an ovenproof non-stick frying pan. Season the breasts with pepper and cook for two minutes over medium heat, until golden, turning to seal all over. Pour in a half-cup water, cover, and cook in the oven for 10–12 minutes or until the chicken is cooked, juicy, and tender.

Remove from the oven, coat with the corn salsa, and serve.

Per serving: 456 Calories, 8g fat, 1g saturated fat, 0.19g sodium

Stuffed chicken paupiettes with smoked ham and corn

I first saw cornflakes used as a coating for chicken when I worked in Dallas, Texas. It led me to think of endless possibilities, from stuffings to corn sauces. Here they make a coating for stuffed chicken rolls. **Serves 4**

4 x 6-ounce chicken breasts, skinless

3 ounces low-fat cream cheese (⅓ cup)

1 garlic clove, crushed

2 tablespoons chopped flat-leaf parsley

¾ cup diced smoked ham

1 small can corn, drained

1 egg yolk

1 cup fresh white breadcrumbs

Good pinch of paprika

Oil-water spray (see page 33)

For the coating

3 ounces cornflakes (about 3½ cups)

¾ cup fresh white breadcrumbs

1¼ ounces flat-leaf parsley (about ¾ cup)

2 tablespoons all-purpose flour

1 egg white, lightly beaten

Preheat the oven to 400°F.

Cut a slit down one side of each chicken breast, ensuring you don't cut right through.

In a bowl, combine the cream cheese, garlic, parsley, ham, corn, egg yolk, and breadcrumbs. Carefully spoon the mixture into each chicken pocket, ensuring it is neat and compact.

To make the coating, place the cornflakes in a blender, add the breadcrumbs and parsley, and blitz until the mix resembles fine crumbs. Transfer to a shallow dish. Carefully coat the chicken breasts with the flour, then the egg white, then finally with the cornflake crumbs.

Place the breasts on a non-stick baking sheet, squirt a little oil-water spray over each one, and bake in the oven for 20–25 minutes or until cooked.

Serve with spinach leaves and boiled new potatoes.

Per serving: 494 Calories, 9g fat, 4g saturated fat, 0.99g sodium

Oven-steamed guinea fowl
The guinea fowl is becoming more popular as a low-fat option. It can be somewhat dry because of its low fat content, but steaming it, as in this recipe, in a foil pouch, keeps it moist and retains all the flavors. Chicken may be used instead, if you prefer. **Serves 4**

4 x 5-ounce guinea fowl breasts, skinless
1 tablespoon chopped cilantro
1 tablespoon chopped marjoram
Juice of 1 lemon
1 tablespoon brown sugar
1 lemon, cut into 8 thin slices
12 asparagus spears

1 teaspoon Dijon mustard
2 tablespoons half-fat crème fraîche (or half-fat sour cream)
3½ ounces black trompette wild mushrooms (or button mushrooms) –about 1 heaped cup
½ cup dry or sweet vermouth

Place the breasts in a dish, sprinkle the cilantro, marjoram, and lemon juice over them, scatter the lime leaves on top, and cover with plastic wrap. Marinate for two hours in the fridge.
Preheat the oven to 400°F.
In a non-stick frying pan, heat the sugar with a quarter-cup water and lightly caramelize it. Add the lemon slices and caramelize on both sides. Set aside.
Cook the asparagus in boiling water for two minutes, remove with a slotted spoon, refresh in cold water, and drain well. Combine the mustard and crème fraîche in a bowl, add the marinated breasts, and mix well together.
Take four sheets of foil, each large enough to wrap a fowl breast. Place a breast on each piece of foil, arrange some mushrooms and asparagus on top, and douse with a little vermouth. Bring up the sides of the foil around the breasts and press the edges together to seal them securely.
Place the pouches on a baking sheet and cook in the oven for 15–20 minutes. Remove and transfer the pouches to four serving dishes. Let your guests open their own pouch at the table to experience the wonderful aromas within, and serve with boiled new potatoes and carrot purée.

Per serving: 244 Calories, 6g fat, 2g saturated fat, 0.13g sodium

Baked poussin (squab chicken) with chili jam and yogurt
This chili jam recipe is taken from my book Raising the Heat. *It has many uses, not only as a dip or relish for Asian foods, but also, as I discovered, as a wonderful spicy topping for baked chicken.* **Serves 4**

4 x 1-pound poussins (squab chickens), with skin removed
For the chili jam
½ cup rice wine vinegar
⅓ cup soft brown sugar
6 tablespoons raisins
2 shallots, finely chopped
1 garlic clove, crushed
7 ounces red chiles, seeded and chopped (about 1½ cups)

½ tablespoon ginger root, chopped
1 teaspoon nam pla (fish sauce)
¼ cup low-fat plain yogurt
2 teaspoons chopped cilantro
½ teaspoon ground turmeric
Freshly ground black pepper
Lime wedges and cilantro, for garnishing

To make the chili jam, place the vinegar and sugar in a pan and bring to a boil slowly to dissolve the sugar. Add the raisins and cook to a light caramel; the liquid should be syrupy. Stir in the shallots, garlic, chiles, ginger, and fish sauce, then remove from the heat and let cool. Place in a blender and blitz to a coarse purée. This can be made in advance and kept in the fridge for up to four weeks.
Preheat the oven to 400°F.
Using a small knife, cut slits into the breasts and legs of the poussins. In a bowl, mix the chili jam, yogurt, chopped cilantro, and turmeric, then rub it on the chickens, ensuring it is rubbed into the slits in each bird.
Place the poussins in a large non-stick baking pan and cook in the oven for 25–30 minutes or until cooked, crisp, and slightly charred all over. Serve garnished with lime wedges and cilantro.

Per serving: 353 Calories, 4g fat, 2g saturated fat, 0.27g sodium

Turkey, porchetta-style, with dried mustard fruits

Porchetta is a wonderful aromatic way of serving pork, Italian style, ideally suckling pig, but sometimes pork loin. Here I use a low-fat alternative, turkey breast, which works equally well. **Serves 8**

8-10 pound free-range turkey, skin and legs removed
1 tablespoon unsaturated oil
½ cup dry white wine
2½ cups chicken stock (see page 39)

For the mustard fruits
⅔ cup sugar
⅔ cup apple juice
11 ounces ready-to-eat dried fruits (apricots, figs, prunes) –about 1¾-2 cups
¼ cup white wine vinegar

2 tablespoons chopped candied lemon peel
1 teaspoon English mustard powder

For the stuffing
3 tablespoons chopped fresh rosemary
2 tablespoons fennel seeds
8 garlic cloves, crushed
Juice and peel of 1 lemon
3 tablespoons chopped marjoram
2 bay leaves
1 tablespoon olive oil

Preheat the oven to 400°F.

To make the stuffing, pulse the ingredients together to a coarse paste in a blender.

Remove the breasts. (Also remove the legs but set aside for another use.) Using a sharp knife, cut a slit in each breast lengthwise about two-thirds of the way along, to form a pocket, ensuring that you do not cut right through.

Open up the meat and, using a kitchen mallet or rolling pin, lightly pound it out. Rub the stuffing paste all over the inside. Close the pockets and tie with kitchen string.

Heat the oil in a large, flameproof, non-stick, baking tray on the stovetop, and seal the turkey all over until golden. Remove from the burner and place the breasts on a wire rack set inside a baking pan so that the fat can drip away. Place in the oven to roast for 50 minutes to one hour, or until the juices run clear when the meat is pierced with a small knife. Be careful not to overcook, since the meat will become dry.

To make the mustard fruits, combine the sugar, apple juice, and a half-cup water in a pan. Stir until the sugar is dissolved. **Add** the fruits and cook over low heat for 20 minutes or until they are soft. Add the vinegar, stir, and cook for a further five minutes, then add the candied lemon peel. Mix well, then stir in the mustard. Let it cool to room temperature.

When the turkey is cooked, remove from the oven and keep warm. Put the flameproof baking pan over a burner, pour in the wine, and boil for two minutes. Add the stock and boil until it is reduced by half. Remove any fat that may rise to the surface using a piece of paper towel.

Cut the turkey into slices, pour the gravy over it, and garnish with the mustard fruits. Serve with roasted butternut squash, broccoli, and roasted new potatoes.

Per serving: 373 Calories, 5g fat, 1g saturated fat, 0.2g sodium

Pheasant casserole with autumn fruits

Pheasant is traditionally roasted, but this game bird also makes a wonderful casserole, although chicken can easily be substituted. Pheasant is best during late autumn and winter – October and December. **Serves 4**

1 oven-ready pheasant, cut into 8 pieces, skin removed
Freshly ground black pepper
2 tablespoons all-purpose flour
1 tablespoon unsaturated oil
¼ cup calvados (apple brandy)
1 cup apple juice
1 tablespoon honey
11 ounces small pearl onions (about 2½-3cups)

3 cups chicken stock (see page 39)
½ tablespoon Dijon mustard
2 celery stalks, thinly sliced
2 Granny Smith apples, peeled, cored, and cut into wedges
1 pear, peeled, cored and cut into wedges
1 bay leaf

Preheat the oven to 350°F.

Place the pheasant pieces in a bowl, season with pepper, sprinkle the flour over them, and mix well.

Heat the oil in a flameproof casserole dish, or heavy, ovenproof pan. Pat the pheasant pieces with a paper towel to remove any excess flour and place them in the pan. Cook over medium heat for four to five minutes or until browned.

Pour in the calvados and cook for one minute. Add the apple juice, honey, and onions, and cook until the mixture becomes slightly syrupy in consistency. Add the chicken stock and mustard and bring to a boil, then add the celery, apple, and pear pieces, and tuck in the bay leaf.

Cover with a lid and cook in the oven for one to one and a half hours or until tender. Discard the bay leaf and serve.

Per serving: 281 Calories, 5g fat, 1g saturated fat, 0.36g sodium

Duck and parsnip pie

I first prepared this variation of a shepherd's pie in England on Carlton TV's Food Daily, *some years ago. The film crew took no time at all to demolish it after filming. It is full of flavor, and duck makes a welcome change from the usual ground lamb.* **Serves 4**

1 tablespoon unsaturated oil
1½ pounds ground duck from 5 duck legs (remove the skin and all visible fat)
1 onion, finely chopped
1 carrot, cut into small dice
½ rutabaga (or turnip), cut into small dice
1 celery stalk, cut into dice
1 garlic clove, crushed
1 tablespoon tomato paste
1 tablespoon all-purpose flour
½ cup hot chicken stock (see page 39)

7 ounces canned tomatoes (¾ cup)
1 teaspoon chopped oregano
1 small bay leaf
1 teaspoon Dijon mustard
2 teaspoons Worcestershire sauce
For the crust
14 ounces parsnips, cut into small chunks (about 3½ cups)
7 ounces potatoes, cut into chunks (about 1½ cups)
1¼ cups low-fat milk

To make the crust. cook the parsnips and potatoes in boiling water for 20–25 minutes or until very tender. Drain. Mash, add the milk, and beat to a smooth purée.

Heat the oil in a non-stick frying pan, then add the ground duck, a little at a time, and fry until sealed and golden. Remove to a colander and let drain to remove any excess fat.

Return the pan to the heat, add the vegetables and garlic, and cook for two to three minutes. Return the meat to the pan, add the tomato paste and cook for one minute. Sprinkle the flour and combine well. Gradually add the stock and tomatoes, and stir until it forms a sauce. Add the herbs, mustard, and Worcestershire sauce, cover, reduce the heat, and cook for 25 minutes.

Preheat the grill to its highest setting.

Transfer the cooked duck mixture to a baking dish and top carefully with the mashed potatoes and parsnips. Broil until the topping is bubbly, golden, and crispy. Let cool slightly before serving with cabbage or steamed carrots.

Per serving: 428 Calories, 16g fat, 4g saturated fat, 0.4g sodium

Grilled balsamic venison steak with green peppercorns and cranberries

Here are tender venison steaks in a hot and spicy, sweet sauce. Other game such as pheasant or partridge would work equally well, as would duck breast. **Serves 4**

4 x 6-ounce venison steaks, cut from the fillet

Freshly ground black pepper

½ teaspoon Chinese five-spice powder

2 tablespoons balsamic vinegar

½ tablespoon honey

Oil-water spray (see page 33)

Parsley, for garnishing

For the sauce

3 tablespoons cranberry jelly

1 tablespoon green peppercorns, drained, rinsed, and dried

2 ounces fresh or frozen cranberries (about ½ cup)

Juice and peel of 1 orange

½ cup good-quality red wine

½ cup beef stock (see page 39)

1 tablespoon balsamic vinegar

Season the venison steaks liberally with the black pepper, then rub in the five-spice powder. Combine the vinegar and honey and brush liberally over the steaks. Set aside.

In a pan, heat all the sauce ingredients together and simmer gently for 10–15 minutes, or until the sauce is reduced and coats the back of a spoon.

Heat a grill pan until very hot, and lightly spray with the oil-water spray. Add the venison steaks and cook over high heat for three to five minutes for medium and pink, or leave them a little longer if you prefer them well done.

Place the steaks on four serving plates and coat with sauce. Scatter the parsley leaves on top, and serve with puréed celeriac.

Per serving: 259 Calories, 3g fat, 0g saturated fat, 0.14g sodium

Bulgogi barbecue pork

Bulgogi is a national dish of Korea and is traditionally stir-fried beef, marinated in soy sauce, with quite a strong, spicy flavor. This is my version – a great barbecue dish during the summer, but actually good at any time.

Serves 4

⅔ cup reduced-salt soy sauce

⅓ cup medium-dry sherry

1-inch piece of fresh ginger root, peeled, finely shredded

2 garlic cloves, crushed

1 tablespoon sesame oil

½ teaspoon dried chili flakes

1 tablespoon brown sugar

1½ pounds lean pork fillet, all fat removed

1 tablespoon lime juice

2 ounces cilantro (about 1-1¼ cups leaves)

In a pan, mix the soy sauce, sherry, ginger, garlic, sesame oil, chili flakes, and sugar, and gently bring to a boil.

Place the pork fillet in a shallow dish, then pour the marinade over it. Cover, and place in the fridge for a minimum of four hours, preferably overnight.

Heat a grill pan on the stove until very hot and almost smoking. Remove the pork fillets from the marinade and drain well. Reserve the marinade.

Cook the pork fillet on the hot grill pan for 10–12 minutes, turning it regularly during this time until it caramelizes.

Meanwhile, bring to a boil the reserved marinade, add the lime juice and cilantro, and cook for two minutes.

To serve, slice the pork into half-inch slices, and coat all over with the sauce.

Serve with noodles or stir-fried rice.

Per serving: 319 Calories, 10g fat, 3g saturated fat, 1.74g sodium

Sicilian-grilled lamb with saffron and raisin polenta

Believe it or not, this sauce is one I prepared for our staff dining room at the hotel. The staff loved it, I am glad to say, and I hope you will, too. The saffron and raisins give the polenta a fragrant flavor. **Serves 4**

1 teaspoon olive oil
2 garlic cloves, crushed
2 shallots, finely chopped
1 tablespoon sherry vinegar
2 teaspoons brown sugar
7 ounces canned tomatoes, chopped (¾ cup)
12 best-quality black olives
¼ cup marsala wine
1 tablespoon superfine capers, drained and rinsed
4 x 6-ounce lean leg of lamb steaks, fat removed
1 teaspoon oregano
2 tablespoons chopped basil

For the polenta
1 garlic clove, crushed
Good pinch of saffron
½ cup skim milk
6 ounces fine cornmeal (polenta) –about 1 heaped cup
¼ cup raisins
2 tablespoons quark (if unavailable, use low-fat sour cream)

To make the polenta, bring 3 cups water to a boil in a pan along with the garlic, saffron, and milk. Carefully pour in the polenta and stir continuously to form a smooth consistency. Add the raisins, then reduce the heat and continue to cook over low heat until the polenta thickens and its consistency resembles that of wet mashed potatoes, this should take about 20–25 minutes. Fold in the quark, and keep warm.

Heat the olive oil in a pan, add the shallots and garlic, and cook over low heat until softened. Add the vinegar, sugar, tomatoes, olives, and marsala wine, and simmer for 10 minutes until reduced in thickness. Then add the capers and keep warm.

Preheat a grill pan and when smoking, add the steaks and sprinkle the oregano and basil on them. Grill for two to three minutes on each side, a little longer if you prefer them more cooked.

Serve the polenta on four serving plates, top with the lamb, pour a little sauce over them, and serve.

Per serving: 517 Calories, 17g fat, 7g saturated fat, 0.49g sodium

Aromatic lamb chops with ginger squash and cilantro sambal

Wonderful for barbecues, this marinade with delicate Indian spices works well on chicken and pork, too. Sambals often accompany rice or curry dishes in Indonesia and Malaysia. **Serves 4**

1 onion, finely chopped
2 garlic cloves, crushed
1 red chile, seeded and finely chopped
1 teaspoon ground cumin
1 teaspoon ground cardamom
½ teaspoon ground turmeric
8 x 3½-ounce large, lean lamb cutlets

For the squash
1-inch piece of fresh ginger root, finely chopped
¼ cup brown sugar
½ cup balsamic vinegar
1½ pounds butternut squash, peeled
Oil-water spray (see page 33)

For the cilantro sambal
2 ounces cilantro (about 1 heaped cup leaves)
1 green chile, seeded and chopped
Juice of ½ lemon
½ small onion, chopped

Preheat the oven to 400°F.

In a bowl, combine the onion, garlic, chile, cumin, cardamom, and turmeric. Rub this mixture on to the cutlets, cover with plastic wrap and let marinate for four hours at room temperature.

In a non-stick frying pan, gently heat the ginger, sugar, and vinegar, until the sugar has dissolved.

Cut the squash into large wedges, place in a roasting pan and spray lightly with the oil-water spray. Place in the oven for 15 minutes until golden in color. Add the ginger balsamic syrup, turn the squash in the syrup, and continue cooking for a further 15 minutes.

Spray a grill pan with the oil-water spray and heat until very hot. Remove the cutlets from the marinade and cook in the pan for three to four minutes on each side until slightly charred.

Meanwhile, to make the sambal, place all the ingredients in a blender and pulse to a coarse texture. Place the grilled cutlets on the squash and serve with a little sambal alongside them.

Per serving: 375 Calories, 13g fat, 6g saturated fat, 0.12g sodium

Honey-glazed ham with chile, plums, and minted rutabaga purée

I am a great lover of ham steaks, although they can be salty. If so, soak them in a little milk for an hour prior to cooking. The rutabaga purée is wonderful in this dish, a lovely accompaniment. **Serves 4**

2 tablespoons honey
1 teaspoon Dijon mustard
1 tablespoon balsamic vinegar
4 thick ham steaks, all visible fat removed
Oil-water spray (see page 33)

For the rutabaga purée
1 large rutabaga, cut into chunks
²/₃ cup low-fat milk
2 tablespoons mint jelly

For the plums
6 large ripe plums, quartered and pitted
2 tablespoons sugar
1 red chile, seeded and finely chopped
2 tablespoons red wine vinegar
Juice of 1 lime

To make the purée, place the rutabaga in a pan, cover with water, and bring to a boil. Cook for 25 minutes or until very soft, then drain. Blend the rutabaga and the milk to a smooth purée, then stir in the mint jelly until dissolved. Set aside, but keep warm.

Mix together the honey, mustard, and vinegar, then brush liberally all over the ham steaks. Heat a ridged grill pan and lightly squirt with the oil-water spray. Add the ham steaks and grill for three to four minutes on each side until cooked.

Place the plums in a pan large enough so they can fit in one layer. In a small pan, dissolve the sugar with a quarter-cup water. Add the chile, heat gently, and cook until the sugar caramelizes to a rich golden color. Remove from the heat, add the vinegar and a half-cup water, and stir until well mixed. Pour this over the plums and cook gently, basting the plums in the syrup as they cook. Add the lime juice and keep warm.

To serve, pile a mound of rutabaga purée on each plate and top with a ham steak and some spicy caramelized plums.

Per serving: 438 Calories, 15g fat, 5g saturated fat, 3.45g sodium

Slow-braised beef with orange, cumin, and olives

This dish comes from Morocco, where it is usually prepared with lamb or mutton. The intense flavors magnify during its long braising time, and the smells as it cooks are tantalizingly good. **Serves 4**

1½ pounds lean chuck steak, all visible fat and sinew removed
1 onion, sliced
2 garlic cloves, crushed
2 carrots, sliced
Peel of 1 orange
2 sprigs of rosemary
1¼ cups orange juice from fresh or concentrate
2 tablespoons unsaturated oil

2 teaspoons ground cumin
One 14½-ounce can tomatoes, chopped
1 tablespoon tomato paste
3 cups beef stock (see page 39)
12 best-quality black olives
1 tablespoon chopped mint
1 tablespoon chopped cilantro
6 tablespoons slivered almonds

A day in advance, cut the meat into 2-inch cubes and place in a large bowl. Add the onion, garlic, carrots, orange peel, and rosemary. Pour the orange juice over it, mix well, then cover and place in the refrigerator overnight.

On the day, preheat the oven to 400°F.

Drain off and reserve the excess liquid from the marinated meat, reserving the vegetables and herbs, too. Dry the meat well with paper towels.

Heat a non-stick flameproof casserole dish or other heavy ovenproof pan until almost smoking, add the oil, and fry the meat, a little at a time, until sealed and golden all over. Remove each batch from the pan and keep warm. To the same pan, add the drained vegetables and herbs from the marinade along with the ground cumin, and cook for two minutes. Add the tomatoes, tomato paste, and reserved orange marinade juices. Add the stock and bring to a boil.

Return the meat to the sauce, cover with a lid, then cook in the oven for one to one and a half hours or until the meat is tender.

Remove from the oven and stir in the olives and fresh herbs, then scatter the almonds over it.

Serve with pilaf-style rice and broccoli.

Per serving: 558 Calories, 22g fat, 4g saturated fat, 0.65g sodium

Poached beef tenderloin with horseradish and caper sauce

We all tend to roast or broil beef, but poaching can be great as well as healthy. I do not suggest using a bouillon cube to make the broth for this dish. Ideally prepare your own, following the recipe on page 39. **Serves 4**

4 cups well-flavored beef stock (see page 39)
1 sprig of thyme
1 small bay leaf
¼ cup dry sherry
4 x 6-ounce beef tenderloin steaks
12 baby carrots
2 celery stalks, cut in 2-inch lengths

12 baby leeks, trimmed
2 turnips, cut into wedges
8 heads of baby fennel

For the sauce
¼ cup low-fat plain yogurt
1 teaspoon grated horseradish
1 tablespoon superfine capers, drained, rinsed, and chopped
2 tablespoons chopped parsley

Heat the beef stock with the thyme, bay leaf, and sherry, in a large pot. Bring to a boil, reduce the heat, and simmer for five minutes.

Heat a non-stick frying pan and, when hot, dry-seal the beef steaks all over, then add to the stock. Cook for 8–10 minutes, then add the vegetables and cook for a further five minutes.

Meanwhile, to make the sauce, combine all the ingredients and mix well.

Remove the beef and cut into thick slices. Arrange in deep bowls, pour over vegetables and stock over them and serve with the horseradish and caper sauce, boiled new potatoes, and Savoy cabbage, if you like.

Per serving: 318 Calories, 12g fat, 5g saturated fat, 0.5g sodium

Charbroiled tenderloin of beef with arugula salsa verde

This sensational dish looks and tastes delicious. Don't worry if fresh pumpkin is out of season, any seasonal squash variety will do. The salsa verde gives the beef a little bite. **Serves 4**

1 pound pumpkin, peeled and cut into wedges (about 4 cups)
1 large head of fennel, cut into wedges
1 tablespoon chopped rosemary,
1½ cups chicken stock (see page 39)
4 x 5-ounce lean tenderloin steaks, fat removed
Freshly ground black pepper
Basil leaves, for garnishing
For the arugula salsa verde
2 oz. arugula leaves (1⅓ cups)

1 ounces basil leaves (about 2 handfuls)
1 tablespoon chopped flat-leaf parsley
1 tablespoon capers, drained, rinsed, and dried
1 garlic clove, crushed
1 tablespoon balsamic vinegar
1 teaspoon Dijon mustard
5 tablespoons hot water
1 level teaspoon olive oil
2 canned anchovy fillets, drained and rinsed

Put the pumpkin, fennel, and rosemary in a heavy saucepan. Pour in the chicken stock until it covers the pumpkin and bring to a boil. Cover, and cook over medium heat for 10–12 minutes. Remove the lid and reduce the heat to a simmer. Continue cooking for about 10 minutes until the vegetables are tender and syrupy. Check the vegetables while they are cooking, adding a little water if they stick to the pan.

To make the salsa verde, put all the ingredients in a blender and pulse until you have a coarse-textured, thick, green sauce.

Season the fillet steaks lightly with pepper and place them on a very hot preheated ridged cast-iron grill pan or barbecue grill. Cook until the steaks are seared and crusty underneath, then turn them over and cook the other side. Allow about three to four minutes each side for rare, four to five minutes for medium, and 7–8 minutes for well done.

Arrange the pumpkin and fennel wedges on four serving plates. Place a fillet steak on top and drizzle some salsa verde over it. Garnish with basil leaves and serve immediately.

Per serving: 261 Calories, 11g fat, 4g saturated fat, 0.39g sodium

5

Desserts

Drunken bananas and kumquats

A simple dessert with a lot of flavor, but no fat! Guests are always intrigued when their food arrives mysteriously wrapped in foil, and there are always suitably appreciative noises when they open them and the aromas are released. **Serves 4**

3 tablespoons apricot jam	4 bananas
2 tablespoons brown sugar	3 ounces kumquats
½ cup dark rum	Quark or low-fat fromage frais,
Juice and peel of 1 orange	or low-fat yogurt, for
1 vanilla bean	serving

Preheat oven to 400°F.

In a pan, combine a half-cup water with the apricot jam, sugar, rum, orange juice and peel, and bring to a boil.

Using a small knife, carefully split the vanilla bean and scrape out the seeds into the pan.

Peel the bananas, but leave them whole. Cut the kumquats in half.

Take four sheets of foil, approximately ten by six inches each, and fold them into shallow boat-shaped pouches.

Place one banana and some kumquats in each piece, then pour the apricot sauce over them. Fold up the sides of each pouch to seal it horizontally. Place on a large baking sheet and cook in the oven for 20 minutes.

Bring to the table and let the guests open the packages themselves. Serve with a generous spoonful of quark or low-fat fromage frais or yogurt.

Per serving: 222 Calories, 0g fat, 0g saturated fat, 0.01g sodium

Baked fruit kabobs on chocolate couscous

You may be surprised to see sweet couscous used as a base for these fruit kabobs, but you'll soon discover that the chocolate works really well and makes an interesting variation. **Serves 4**

	For the couscous
2 oranges	1 cup skim milk
2 bananas	1 teaspoon ground cinnamon
1 ripe pear	3 tablespoons sugar
4 pitted prunes, soaked and	½ tablespoon cocoa powder
cut in half	½ cup couscous
¼ cup sugar	½ cup rum (optional)
2 tablespoons rum (optional)	

For the couscous, heat the milk, cinnamon, and sugar in a small saucepan, add the cocoa, stir well, and bring to a boil. Place the couscous in a bowl, pour the chocolate milk over it, stir well, then cover and let stand for five to eight minutes. Separate the grains of couscous with a fork, cover, and leave for a further five minutes. Stir once again, add the rum, if using, and leave in the fridge.

Soak four bamboo skewers in cold water, for about 30 minutes.

Preheat the oven to 450°F.

Peel the oranges, bananas, and pear. Cut each banana into eight thick slices; cut the oranges into quarters. Cut the pear in half, remove the core, then cut into quarters.

Thread the fruit on to the skewers, with the prune halves at each end of the skewers. Place the fruit skewers in a shallow ovenproof dish.

In a pan, boil the sugar with a quarter-cup water for five minutes to make a syrup. Pour this over the skewers, leaving a little aside for basting, and douse with rum, if using. Bake in the oven for five minutes, basting occasionally with syrup.

Serve the chilled couscous topped with the fruit kebabs, pouring any remaining syrup over them. Fruit sorbet or vanilla ice cream makes a lovely accompaniment.

Per serving: 304 Calories, 1g fat, 0g saturated fat, 0.05g sodium

Chocolate and banana "gratin" *Here's a dish with a flavor that is reminiscent of my childhood when I used to eat banana splits. Bananas baked with rich chocolate — delicious. This custard has been created along the same lines and is very simple to make.* **Serves 4**

3 large egg yolks
½ cup condensed skim milk
½ cup skim milk

3 tablespoons chocolate milk-shake flavouring
1 large banana
4 teaspoons sugar

Preheat the oven to 300°F.

Whisk the egg yolks together with both milks and the chocolate flavoring until creamy. Strain through a fine mesh strainer into a bowl.

Divide the mixture into four small ramekins. Place in a roasting pan, then fill the roasting pan with hot water until the water reaches halfway up the sides of the ramekins.

Cook in the oven for 45–50 minutes, remove from the oven, and cool. If you like, you can keep the custards in the fridge once cooled, until needed.

To serve, peel the banana and cut into thick slices. Arrange slices on top of the custards so that they overlap.

Sprinkle the caster sugar evenly over the bananas, then place under a preheated broiler until golden and caramelized, or use a kitchen blowtorch.

Let cool slightly before serving.

Per serving: 228 Calories, 5g fat, 1g saturated fat, 0.06g sodium

Strawberry romanoff *A great dessert during the summer when strawberries are at their best, cheap, plentiful, and fragrant. There are French, Russian, and American versions of this dish and a true Romanoff will also include a liqueur. Try serving with ice cream.* **Serves 4**

One 6-ounce package of strawberry jello
7 ounces strawberries, cut into pieces (about 1½ cups)
1²/₃ cups nonfat dry milk
¼ cup half-fat crème fraîche or half-fat sour cream
2 tablespoons roughly chopped mint, plus whole mint leaves for garnishing

For the cookies
5 tablespoons reduced-fat spread
A scant ½ cup sugar
2 egg whites
6 tablespoons all-purpose flour, sifted
Oil-water spray (see page 33)

To make the romanoff, prepare the jello following the instructions on the package. Let it cool to just warm.

Place half of the strawberries in a blender, blitz to a purée, and set aside.

Mix the milk powder into the warm jello and, using a hand-held mixer, whip the jello until it becomes airy in texture. Fill four tumbler-style glasses with the jello mixture until they are three-quarters full, then place in the refrigerator to set.

Mix the remaining strawberries with the crème fraîche and chopped mint.

Preheat the oven to 375°F.

To make the cookies, beat the spread, sugar, and egg whites in a bowl with an electric mixer until pale in color. Stir in the flour.

Lightly grease a baking tray with a squirt of oil-water spray. Place the mixture in a pastry bag and, using a half-inch tube, pipe eight 3-inch lengths on the baking tray. Bake for five to six minutes or until the edges are brown and the cookies cooked. Let cool before serving.

To serve, remove the Romanoff from the fridge, top with the crème fraîche and strawberries, pour the strawberry purée over it, and garnish with the cookies and whole mint leaves.

Per serving: 504 Calories, 9g fat, 3g saturated fat, 0.39g sodium

Pears in port and cranberry syrup

The colors in this dish are amazing: scarlet red pears in a contrasting syrup. A dish that is sure to impress, and ideal for autumn and winter entertaining when pears are at their best.

Serves 4

4 large firm but ripe pears (Bartlett, Comice)	½ cinnamon stick
1¼ cups cranberry juice	2 cups fresh or frozen cranberries
½ cup port	Sprigs of mint, for garnishing
A scant ½ cup sugar	Buttermilk and lemon sorbet (see page 154), for serving
Peel of 1 orange	

Using a potato peeler, peel the pears neatly, leaving the stalks intact and retaining the shape of the fruit. Cut a little off the bottom of each pear to help it remain upright during poaching.

Choose a saucepan that will hold the four pears upright side by side. Place the cranberry juice, port, sugar, orange peel and cinnamon in the pan and bring to a boil, stirring, until the sugar has dissolved. Add the pears, cover the pan, and simmer for 20–25 minutes or until the pears are tender when pierced with a knife, but still retaining their shape.

Using a slotted spoon, remove the pears from the syrup and let cool. Add the cranberries to the syrup and boil rapidly until reduced by two thirds. Let cool, then pour the syrup and cranberries over the pears and place in the refrigerator for up to four hours to chill thoroughly.

Garnish with mint and serve with the Buttermilk and Lemon Sorbet, although low-fat vanilla yogurt would make a good alternative.

Per serving: 233 Calories, 0g fat, 0g saturated fat, 0.02g sodium

Coffee marsala nectarines with crème fraîche

For me, coffee and Marsala wine are natural flavor partners. They instill a sweet yet bitter flavor that works so well. This is an elegant, sophisticated dish, perfect for a dinner party. **Serves 4**

8 ripe but firm nectarines	1 cinnamon stick
A scant ½ cup sugar	¼ cup Marsala wine
1 tablespoon coffee-flavored syrup	½ cup half-fat crème fraîche or half-fat sour cream, for serving
1 vanilla bean, split in two	

Preheat the oven to 350°F.

Blanch the nectarines in boiling water for one minute, remove, and refresh quickly in cold water, then peel the skins.

Cut the nectarines in half, remove the pits and place the fruit in a baking pan.

Boil one and a quarter cups water with the sugar, and cook for 10 minutes to form a light syrup. Add the coffee syrup, vanilla, cinnamon, and Marsala wine. Pour it over the nectarines and bake, uncovered, for 25 minutes, until the nectarines are cooked, basting regularly.

Remove the spices and vanilla from the syrup.

Using a slotted spoon, lift out the fruit to a dish and let it cool. Pour the remaining syrup into a pan and reduce over a high heat by one third of its volume. Pour it over the nectarines and let cool completely. Chill overnight in the syrup, and serve with crème fraîche.

Per serving: 255 Calories, 4g fat, 2g saturated fat, 0.04g sodium

Apple and cherry baklava with cinnamon syrup

Baklava is a speciality of Greece and the Middle East. Normally the phyllo pastry is full of crunchy nuts, baked, and then drizzled with warm syrup; here I have come up with an apple and cherry variation. **Serves 4**

2 Granny Smith apples

¼ cup raisins

2½ tablespoons sugar

5 ounces cherries, pitted (about ⅔ cup)

½ cup walnut halves, chopped

½ cup almonds, chopped

1 teaspoon ground cinnamon

⅛ teaspoon ground cloves

3 ounces fresh brioche crumbs (or bread crumbs) –about

1½-2 cups

3 phyllo pastry dough sheets

2 egg whites, lightly beaten

Low-fat fromage frais, yogurt or half-fat crème fraîche, for serving

For the syrup

A scant ½ cup sugar

Peel and juice of ½ lemon

2 tablespoons honey

½ teaspoon ground cinnamon

Preheat the oven to 400°F.

Peel the apples, remove the cores, and cut into large chunks. Place in a pan along with the raisins, sugar, and a quarter cup water. Cover and cook over medium heat for 8–10 minutes, until the apples are soft but not mushy and no liquid remains.

Place the apples in a bowl and let cool. Add the cherries, nuts, spices, and crumbs, and bind the whole mix together well.

Lay one sheet of phyllo on a flat surface, brush with egg white. Top with a second sheet, brush, then top with the last sheet, brushing again with egg white. Cut the phyllo to form four squares.

Divide the apple and cherry mix between the four squares, then bring up the sides of each to form a pouch and scrunch the top to seal in the apple filling.

Brush over each pouch with egg white, then place on a baking sheet and bake for 12–15 minutes until golden.

Meanwhile, prepare the syrup. Place the sugar with a half cup water in a pan and stir over low heat until dissolved. Add the lemon peel and juice, honey, and cinnamon, then boil for six to eight minutes. Remove from the heat and let cool.

Spoon the syrup over the baklava and serve.

Per serving: 554 Calories, 17g fat, 2g saturated fat, 0.39g sodium

Gingersnap bread pudding

Ever since my working days at London's Dorchester Hotel under chef Anton Mosimann, I have loved the bread and butter pudding we prepared lovingly to this recipe. I have created lots of variations on it over the years, well here's another. **Serves 4**

2 tablespoons maple syrup

10 slices of white bread, crusts removed

4 ounces dried figs (about 10)

4 ounces dried apricots (about ½ cup)

3 ounces gingersnaps, crushed (about 6)

A scant ½ cup slivered almonds, toasted

3 cups skim milk

2 large eggs from free-range hens

3 tablespoons sugar

1 vanilla bean, split, seeds removed

¼ cup amaretto (almond liqueur; optional)

¼ cup reduced-sugar apricot jam, warmed

Confectioners' sugar for dusting

Preheat the oven to 300°F.

Brush the maple syrup over the bread slices, then cut the bread into large cubes and place in a bowl. Add the dried fruits, crushes gingersnaps, and toasted almonds. Scatter the bread and fruit evenly over the bottom of a two and a half pint ovenproof dish.

In a bowl, whisk together the milk, eggs, sugar, vanilla, and amaretto, if using. Pour the milk mixture over the fruit and bread, ensuring all the bread is immersed in the milk.

In the oven, heat a large roasting pan containing enough water so that it will come halfway up the sides of the ovenproof dish.

Place the ovenproof dish in the water of the roasting pan and bake the pudding in the oven for 45–50 minutes, until the top is lightly golden and it is just set. Remove and let cool slightly, then brush all over with the warmed apricot jam. Dust with confectioners' sugar and serve warm.

Per serving: 619 Calories, 16g fat, 3g saturated fat, 0.72g sodium

Cherimisu
This dish is my humorous take on tiramisu, *the classic Italian dessert, but without mascarpone, and this variation will soon become a favorite in your home. Leaf gelatin can be hard to find, so, as a guide, a one ounce (25g) package of granulated gelatin equals four leaves.* **Serves 4**

¼ cup kahlúa (coffee-flavored liqueur)
3 tablespoons maraschino (cherry liqueur)
¼ cup brown sugar
¼ cup sugar
3 gelatin leaves
2 cups low-fat cream cheese or quark
Peel of ½ orange
Peel of ½ lemon
12 boudoir cookies (or ladyfingers)
¼ cup coffee syrup mixed with ½ cup boiling water
14 ounces canned morello cherries in syrup, well drained (about 1⅓ cups)
2 teaspoons cocoa powder, for dusting

Warm the liqueurs together in a pan along with the sugars, until hot. Add the gelatin leaves and stir well until dissolved. Set aside to cool.

In a bowl, combine the cheese with the lemon and orange peel, and stir in the liqueur mix.

Soak the boudoir cookies in the coffee syrup mixture for three to four minutes, then arrange a layer of the biscuits in a serving dish, followed by a layer of cheese mix. Scatter some drained cherries over them and repeat the layers until the ingredients are used up.

Dust the top with the cocoa powder, and chill for up to four hours before serving.

Per serving: 387 Calories, 2g fat, 1g saturated fat, 0.12g sodium

Caramelized pineapple and strawberries, with anise and saffron syrup
I go through phases when I use a particular ingredient regularly. Star anise is one favorite that I am using at present in dishes from desserts to sauces and sorbets. **Serves 4**

¼ cup dry white wine
A scant ¼ cup sugar
2-inch piece of orange peel
3 star anise
1 vanilla bean
Pinch of saffron
2 tablespoons Pernod (or other anise-style liqueur)
4 slices of fresh pineapple
7 ounces strawberries, cut in half
Low-fat vanilla ice cream, for serving

Place a half cup water in a pan along with the wine and two-thirds of the sugar, and bring to a boil slowly to dissolve the sugar.

Add the orange peel, star anise, vanilla bean, and saffron, simmer gently for 15–20 minutes until the syrup has thickened slightly, then strain through a wire mesh strainer.

In a non-stick pan, heat the remaining sugar and the Pernod, and caramelize lightly. Add the pineapple and strawberries, and caramelize in the sugar. Pour the syrup over them and cook for two minutes.

Serve warm, with the ice cream.

Per serving: 173 Calories, 0g fat, 0g saturated fat, 0.01g sodium

Not-so-humble black crumble

I truly believe that some of the best desserts in the world originate in the UK. In fact, during my travels, I have seen many chefs trying to recreate British favorites, such as the legendary apple crumble. Here is one I concocted with a low-fat regime in mind. **Serves 4**

¼ cup sugar

5 ounces firm ripe plums, cut in half (about ¾-1 cup)

7 ounces black figs, quartered

1 cup blackberries

1 cup blueberries

For the topping

¾ cup all-purpose flour

1 tablespoon cocoa powder

½ teaspoon ground cinnamon

2 tablespoons brown sugar

¼ cup low-fat spread

3 ounces amaretti cookies, finely crushed (about ¾ cup)

Preheat the oven to 400°F.

To make the topping, place the flour, cocoa powder, cinnamon, sugar, and low-fat spread in a bowl. Mix well, then add the amaretti cookies.

In a pan, add the sugar to a half-cup water and heat until it forms a light syrup. Add the plums and poach for five minutes, then remove from the heat and add the remaining fruits.

Place the fruits in a two and a half cup ovenproof dish. Sprinkle the crumble topping over them and bake in the oven for 15–20 minutes, until golden and crispy.

Serve with low-fat fromage frais or low-fat custard, if you like.

Per serving: 325 Calories, 8g fat, 2g saturated fat, 0.22g sodium

Peanut butter cheesecake tart

In this cheesecake recipe, the graham crackers form a coating on the top of the tart rather than on the bottom. If you can't find leaf gelatin, see the note in the introduction to Cherimisu on page 150 for the granulated gelatin equivalent. **Serves 8**

⅔ cup smooth peanut butter

1½ cups low-fat cream cheese or quark

Peel of 1 orange

3 tablespoons rum

¼ cup sugar

½ cup low-fat milk

4 gelatin leaves, soaked in cold water until soft, then drained

2 egg whites

1 x 8-inch prepared pie shell

For the topping

2 ounces graham crackers (about 8 or 9 crackers)

2 tablespoons honey

In a blender, combine the peanut butter, cheese, orange peel, rum, and sugar, and puree until smooth, then transfer to a bowl. Heat the milk until hot, then add the soaked gelatin. Let cool, then stir into the cheese mixture.

Beat the egg whites until stiff peaks form, and fold into the mixture. Pour into the prepared pie shell and level off to a smooth surface. Place in the refrigerator to set overnight.

Preheat the oven to 350°F.

To make the topping, crush the graham crackers coarsely and mix with the honey. Place on a baking sheet and cook for 15–20 minutes, until the graham crackers and honey slightly caramelize. Let cool, then pulse in a blender until they resemble fine crumbs.

Dust the cheesecake tart with the crumbs and serve with a low-fat ice cream or ice milk.

Per serving: 353 Calories, 19g fat, 5g saturated fat, 0.26g sodium

Low-fat sorbets

Here are a few of my favorite low-fat sorbets based on simple ingredients. They are easy to prepare, but work best when you use a sorbet machine. There are some reasonably priced machines on the market now, and they are well worth the investment. **Serves** 4

Raspberry and vodka sorbet

13 ounces fresh or frozen raspberries, defrosted if frozen (about 2½ cups)	¼ cup vodka
	1⅔ cups sugar

Place the raspberries and vodka in a blender and puree until smooth, then strain through a fine mesh strainer.

Put the sugar and one and a half cups water in a pan, slowly bring to a boil, then reduce the heat and simmer for 10 minutes or until the mixture becomes a thick syrup. Let cool, add the raspberries and vodka, and mix well. Place in a sorbet or ice cream machine, and freeze according to the manufacturer's instructions.

Per serving: 429 Calories, 0g fat, 0g saturated fat, 0.01g sodium

Buttermilk and lemon sorbet

1 cup, 2 tablespoons sugar	Juice and peel of 1 lemon
2¼ cups buttermilk	1 tablespoon honey

Put the sugar and a cup of water in a pan. Slowly bring to a boil, then remove from the heat. Pour into a bowl and chill in the fridge for an hour.

In a bowl, whisk together the buttermilk, lemon juice and peel, and honey. Slowly add the syrup. Place in a sorbet or ice cream machine, and freeze according to the manufacturer's instructions.

Per serving: 304 Calories, 1g fat, 0g saturated fat, 0.08g sodium

Passion fruit and lime sorbet

1⅔ cups sugar	13 ounces fresh passion fruit pulp and seeds (about 2-2½ cups)
Juice of 2 limes	

Put the sugar and a cup and a half of water in a pan, slowly bring to a boil, then reduce the heat and simmer for 10 minutes or until the mixture becomes a thick syrup.

Let cool, add the lime juice and passion fruit, and mix well. Place in a sorbet or ice cream machine, and freeze according to the manufacturer's instructions.

Per serving: 404 Calories, 0g fat, 0g saturated fat, 0.02g sodium

Ricotta sorbet

1 cup, 2 tablespoons sugar	2 tablespoons honey
1¼ pounds ricotta cheese (about 2½ cups)	

Put the sugar and a cup of water in a pan. Slowly bring to a boil, then remove from the heat. Pour into a bowl and chill in the fridge for one hour.

Place the ricotta and honey in a food processor and slowly blend in the chilled syrup. Place in a sorbet or ice cream machine, and freeze according to the manufacturer's instructions.

Per serving: 502 Calories, 18g fat, 11g saturated fat, 0.17g sodium

Layered summer pudding

A real treat at any time. A friend's wife gave me the idea of using a fruit jello instead of gelatin, to bind it. It really is simple and easy to prepare, and my version is layered rather than molded.

Serves 8

1½ pounds mixed summer fruits (e.g., black currants, red currants, strawberries, raspberries)

A scant ½ cup sugar

2 tablespoons crème de cassis (black currant liqueur; optional)

1 package raspberry or strawberry jello

½ loaf sliced white bread, crusts removed

Remove the stalks from the currants. Trim the tops from the strawberries, then cut the strawberries in half.

Place all the fruits except the raspberries in a pan, along with the sugar, and add a cup and a half of water and the cassis liqueur, if using. Simmer gently for five minutes, then add the raspberries and cook for a further two minutes.

Remove from the heat and drain the fruits from the liquid. Set aside the fruits and return the liquid to a boil. Stir in the jello and remove from the heat. Stir until all the jello powder has dissolved. Let cool, then chill in the fridge for 10 minutes or until the jello starts to thicken but not set. Remove the jello from the fridge and mix the chilled jello with the fruits again.

Cut the bread slices in half and place a layer on the bottom of a small gratin dish, with the slices overlapping. Place some of the fruits over the bread and level off. Top with a second layer of bread, then more fruits, finishing with a layer of bread.

Push down the bread to ensure it is immersed in the juices, cover the dish with foil, and place in the fridge for up to four hours to set firm.

To serve, cut out sections of the pudding and serve with a low-fat cream or ice cream.

Per serving: 161 Calories, 0g fat, 0g saturated fat, 0.11g sodium

Index

Resources

US

American Heart Association
National Center
7272 Greenville Avenue
Dallas
TX 75231
1-800-AHA-USA-1 (1-800-242-8721)
www.americanheart.org

National Heart, Lung, and Blood Institute
NHLBUI Health Information Center
Attention: Website
P.O. Box 30105
Bethesda
MD 20824-0105
301-592-8573
240-629-3255 (TTY)
www.nhlbi.nih.gov

Heart Information Network
Heartinfo.org
c/o Trigenesis Communications
26 Main Street
Chatham
NJ 07928
www.heartinfo.org

Heart Center Online
One South Ocean Boulevard
Suite 201
Boca Raton
FL 33432
www.heartcenteronline.com

Heart Point
www.heartpoint.com

CANADA

Heart and Stroke Foundation of Canada
1825 Park Road S.E.
Calgary, Alberta
T2G 3Y6
(403) 264 5549
www.heartandstroke.ca

UK

H·E·A·R·T UK
7 North Road
Maidenhead, Berkshire
SL6 1PE
England
44 (0)1628 628 638
www.heartuk.org.uk

AUSTRALIA

National Heart Foundation of Australia
Cnr. Denison St. & Geils Court
Deakin
ACT 2600
1300 36 27 87
www.heartfoundation.com.au

Acknowledgements

With special thanks to the following people who have made this book possible: to Linda Tubby for her inspired food styling and to Pete Cassidy for the magnificent photographs. Penny Markham for the props, Lara King for her patience and good nature with recipe typing, and Carl Hodson for his design. Not forgetting Kyle and project editor Muna Reyal for all her support, always being at the end of the telephone for me, when I needed her, and most of all for her encouragement. PG